# A HARLOT'S CRY

### ONE WOMAN'S THIRTY-FIVE-YEAR JOURNEY THROUGH THE SEX INDUSTRY

by Mary Frances

with Jennifer Bell

330 Publications LLC
Louisville, KY

330 Publications LLC
PO Box 32301
Louisville, KY 40232
www.330publications.com

Scriptures taken from the Holy Bible, New International Version®, NIV®. Copyright © 1973, 1978, 1984, 2011 by Biblica, Inc.™ Used by permission of Zondervan. All rights reserved worldwide. www.zondervan.com The "NIV" and "New International Version" are trademarks registered in the United States Patent and Trademark Office by Biblica, Inc.™

Cover photos by Firm Anchor Photography
Hair and makeup by Julia Sanders at J.R.'s Spa and Salon
Cover design by Rebecca Sterling at Sterling Design Studio
Book layout ©2017 BookDesignTemplates.com
Proofreading by Allison Lutes

A Harlot's Cry / Mary Frances with Jennifer Bell -- 1st ed.
ISBN 978-1947640009

*In memory of Nana,*
*who was always there for us*

# Contents

# Content Warning and Disclaimer

## Content Warning

This book recounts events and settings that may be upsetting to some readers, including descriptions of violence, neglect, foul language, drug use, unsanitary places, animal abuse, child abuse, sexual abuse, trafficking, and rape. We have attempted to treat these matters truthfully but without the intent to sensationalize or use unnecessarily graphic or salacious language. Please be advised before reading further.

## Disclaimer

The author has attempted to write a truthful account of the events described in this book. Several scenes have been reconstructed from memory. Where possible, we have corroborated details with newspaper articles, official documents, and eye-witness accounts. That being said, we acknowledge that memory is imperfect and perception is subjective; thus, there is always a chance that others may remember or perceive some events, people, or places differently than what the author has communicated here.

In addition, the author does not seek to comment on the present-day character or operations of the people and organizations described in this book. Rather, she only wishes to communicate her perception of and dealings with these people and organizations at a fixed point in time. Laws change, organizations change, and people change, and the author does not intend or desire any harm or ill effect on anyone in the present day.

Several names and descriptions have been changed for the privacy of those involved.

# CHAPTER ONE

# The Baby

They called me "the baby," the last of my mother's fifteen children to survive infancy. Even long into my adult years, my father made certain to introduce me as "the baby," as if I were a prize my parents had waited for after fourteen children. Although many families would indeed view a new baby as a blessing, my parents received each of their children with a mixture of stress and panic. One more mouth to feed, one more back to clothe, one more spot taken up in the shared bed. So great was their desperation that they took to giving away or even selling some of their children to rich families who wanted to rescue children out of poverty. I'm not sure why I was an exception to this practice, but it was into this world of poverty and strain that I entered in August of 1960.

Just as it was a miracle that my parents decided to keep me, so too was it a miracle that I survived my first days on Earth. I was born premature, and the odds of survival were slim for an infant belonging to an impoverished family in Kentucky in those days. I weighed less than four pounds and was brought home from the hospital in a shoebox. My mother dressed me in my cousin Dolores's doll clothes, and I wore my father's old handkerchiefs for diapers. My mother consumed alcohol during all her pregnancies as if the occasional beer was necessary for us while we were in the womb. This was a common behavior at the time—to drink and smoke during pregnancy— and although I escaped the ravages of fetal alcohol syndrome, this wouldn't be the last time my mother's drinking threatened my well-being.

The 1960s were an era of change itself. The Vietnam War was taking hold, and the leaders who were trying to make the world better were being assassinated. Pain was everywhere, and our family dwelled in the poorest of Louisville's ghettos. It was made up of all races, but in spite of our differences in culture and creed, the majority of our community had one thing in common: We were all poor. And in my eyes, we weren't different at all.

Although man had made it to the moon and people all over the country were protesting for change, there was no change in our world. Everything remained the same—the same poverty, the same violence and alcoholism that created despicable circumstances, the same dysfunction and loneliness. Throughout life, I would reach for change, not knowing what I was seeking—just anything other than what I had been born into. For the most part, there was no opportunity to be anything other than what we were—impoverished, uneducated, and without the knowledge of God. But something within my entire being cried out for more than what I had been dealt.

In those days, we lived in a three-room, run-down shotgun house. When you stood at the front door, you could see straight through the whole house to the backyard where the outhouse stood. The walls were grim with old photographs of deceased family members and a few portraits of Jesus. The floors were uneven wooden planks that often gave us splinters, as we rarely wore shoes.

My uncle slept in the front room, where there was a coal stove that we depended on to keep us warm during the winter. The smoke from the stove caked over the front window so that very little light shone through. The house smelled like stale liquor, urine, and vomit, as my uncle often used a bucket as a toilet when he got sick from drinking too much.

The middle room was reserved for us kids. Our mother slept on the floor on blankets while we slept in the bed, sometimes five or six of us crammed together.

The kitchen contained an old, scratched wooden table with only two worn-out chairs, so that our whole family could never fit at once. A single bare lightbulb hung from a wire through the ceiling over the table, and a wringer washer that smelled of mildew stood in the corner. The stench from the outhouse in the backyard also reeked through the kitchen. My aunt used to bathe me in a metal washtub on the floor, and the rest of the family washed themselves using the kitchen sink, drawing the ragged curtains that hung from the doorway in the kitchen for privacy.

My earliest memories do not include many of my brothers and sisters because by the time I came along, most of them had left home by way of prison, adoption, extended family members, and the Vietnam War. No matter how many left, however, my parents were always overwhelmed by the number of mouths to feed. Hopelessness ruled over us, and hunger and shame dictated our lives. To this day, I'm not sure why my parents decided to keep me, and even as a child, I wondered why I had been brought into the world when my parents clearly had neither food nor love to spare.

For many of us in the ghetto, domestic violence was a way of life and yet was something no one ever spoke about. I saw firsthand how poverty bred frustration and short tempers that parents unleashed in front of their children without a second thought for the children's well-being. In our house, my father carried on this grand tradition, and I witnessed not only my father's abuse of my mother, but also my grown brothers beating their wives.

The first time I recall wanting to intervene in the violence was when I saw it happen to one of my sisters. One day while she was visiting my parents, her boyfriend showed up and hit her in the face so hard that blood poured from her nose. I remember her hanging her head over the arm of the chair as blood puddled on the floor. She was in her last trimester of pregnancy with her first child.

After the incident, I guarded the house with a broom as I waited for her boyfriend's return. I marched up and down the sidewalk feeling hurt for her, anger toward him, and a great deal of bravery in my five-year-old body. There was no refuge for women then—no shelter and no police involvement until someone died. I promised myself that when I grew up, I was not going to live the life I was witnessing all around me.

Fights and violence broke out in my parents' house at least once a week and at times went on for days. Friends and extended family all participated, taking out the stresses of life on one another, and inevitably someone—usually my mother—turned over the kitchen table in the heat of argument. Throughout the night, beer bottles and other glass objects could be heard crashing against the floor, often accompanied by the thump of a body. Everyone screamed obscenities, and the blood of whoever was fighting could be found smeared about the house the following morning.

On nights like this, I would hide wherever I could find shelter in that tiny house. My go-to spot was behind piles of dirty clothes in the closet. When it was safe, I would tiptoe out barefoot, careful not to step on the broken beer bottles and dirty dishes shattered on the floor. Whoever stuck around after all the drinking and fighting usually ended up passed out on the floor, and I would have to climb over them to make my way to the bathroom. The smell of whiskey, beer, and cigarette smoke lay heavy in the air, and there was never any food to be found.

My mother often left during these fights, and many times, I awoke to an empty house wondering when she would return. I pleaded with my mother not to drink beer, because I knew what would take place once she got drunk. My mother was five feet tall but had very strong arms from the housework and mounds of ironing she often did for others to earn money. She seemed sad and haggard; she never wore makeup or nice clothes, and she fought depression throughout her life. However, when intoxicated, she could be—and often was—a cruel, sarcastic, and belligerent person who enjoyed inflicting pain on others.

I remember standing next to her at the kitchen table whenever she opened a beer. In the place where most families had dinner and talked about their days, I begged her, "Please let this one be your only beer, Mama." Or I would ask, "Is this the last one, Mama?" She would ignore me or tell me to shut up and go away. When it was apparent that she was beyond intoxicated, I gave up and found a safe place to hide or begged sober family members to take me home with them.

Yet even if I went home with other people, I often witnessed some other form of violence at their houses. But at least at these places, unlike at my house, I knew I would be fed. As young as five years old, I knew better than the adults what was going to happen when they drank, and the strange thing about it was that the next day they acted as though nothing had happened the night before. I watched as the alcohol and drugs helped ease the pain of almost everyone around me but in turn caused another type of pain that no one seemed to notice.

For me, alcohol became my first source of anxiety—the first among many. Detecting the smell of alcohol or a change in the tone and volume of someone's voice would send me into panic. Even the sight of liquor made me a bundle of nerves, and I rarely slept at night out of fear of what was bound to happen. My first anxiety attack happened when I was as young as four years old. I remember telling my mother through tears that I couldn't breathe and was going to die. It was an overwhelming fear that I carried throughout life, a memory so vivid that it still feels like it happened yesterday.

I came to hate this constant fear, even as I hated the hatred building up inside me. I stuck it all deep within my heart, as deep as it would go. But sometimes it would show its face when I acted out during the times my family was sober. Anytime someone tried to touch me, even out of genuine affection, I would rip myself away and scream, "Get your clawy hands away from me! Don't touch me!" I wouldn't share toys with my nieces and nephews and would scream at them at the slightest provocation until they cried. By being mean and hateful, I felt I could overcome the fear.

But under all the anger, I was a tenderhearted child who tried to be a peacemaker in the chaos around me. At an early age, I started refereeing my family's late-night brawls and mediating their screaming matches. Then when it became too violent for a five-year-old to lecture about love in a kitchen full of drunken adults, I would find one of my trustworthy hiding spots.

While most little girls my age played with dolls, I listened to music to cope with my troubles. The bar at the corner, called Clay and Jeff, had a jukebox that we could hear all the way down the street. It played the same music throughout the night, and I would sit at the window straining to hear it as it faded in and out whenever the bar's patrons came and went through the front doors.

My uncle's kitchen was the first place I heard the sound of a phonograph. I used to drag a chair over to where it sat high up on a table. Once there, I turned the crank to wind it and played "Sunshine, Lollipops, and Rainbows" over and over again. I would stand on the kitchen chair and belt out the lyrics as if I actually had a voice.

As young as I was, everything about my household had forced me to mature emotionally in ways I wasn't ready for, and hearing that music was the first time I recall finding peace and even joy in the midst of everything around me. It allowed me to escape to a place where I didn't have to walk on pins and needles or worry about who was on the verge of throwing the next punch.

In the front room listening to me was my cousin Dolores, who had caught polio as a baby. She was almost twelve years old and had gone through surgery on her right knee, leaving her temporarily bedridden while other children played in the streets outside her window. I ran back and forth from the kitchen to the front room to talk to her and pester her with questions about her condition. I pointed at the leg brace propped up in the corner of the room and asked, "How did you break your leg?" She would gently explain that she hadn't broken her leg but had polio.

Even then, I sensed that Dolores had a strong spirit, and later I would learn to draw from her quiet power. Like me, Dolores was petite, and she had ringlets of black curls that seemed to smother her head. Her eyes were a piercing blue. I admired her beauty and was touched by her gentleness and strength.

Dolores came to stay with us for a time after another surgery that left her in a body cast. Even though she was bedridden, I delighted in her calm and compassionate company in the midst of the drunken brawls and arguments that marked so much of our family. My father, however, soon decided that Dolores was too much of a burden and ordered her out of the house. While I watched in horror, one of my brothers and an uncle carried her on an army stretcher through the park to emergency housing in the Clarksdale Projects just blocks away. My mother never said a word.

It was then I began to seriously question my father's integrity and compassion, but little did I know that it was only a hint of how cruel he could be. Although Dolores didn't live with us anymore, she remained a part of my life and tried desperately to teach me about life, education, and freedom. She never gave up on me, even when I couldn't comprehend her words or focus after a long night of my parents' drunken fights.

Even as the 1960s changed the face of our country, none of that change reached the ghetto. As the world shifted around us, my family continued to live out our dysfunctional lives, all the while grooming me to accept the exploitation that was careening down my path.

# CHAPTER TWO

# Guarantees

Life outside my home began at the Wesley House Community Center. Located in the center of Butchertown, the neighborhood where we lived, Wesley House served those in need in our community, hosted Christmas parties, and provided arts and crafts, a skating rink, and even summer camp for children. The majority of the neighborhood children were members, and there were always classes and activities for people from all walks of life.

For me, Wesley House was heaven on Earth, a warm place that smelled of clean wood as soon as you entered. No alcohol was there to start fights, food came at the same time every day, and the daycare staff's attention was always on us kids. The heartache started only when it was time to go home.

When the activities at the daycare ended and parents picked up their children, I was often left behind. I waited by the door as it swung open, looking out for a familiar face and then deflating when I saw it was another child's parent. The other children smiled and ran to the door when their mommy or daddy showed up to embrace them with kisses and dress them warm, to take them to the places I dreamed to go.

One by one, all my playmates disappeared as their parents

came to pick them up. Then, once again, I would be the last child left, and often underdressed or wearing out-of-season clothes, I would have to walk through the streets in the cold and snow or rain to find my parents.

One of the workers at Wesley House was a sweet, elderly black woman who took pity on me during these humiliating episodes. She knew if she could find my parents anywhere, it would not be at our home, but in one of the local bars. Often she retrieved gloves and warm clothes for me from the donation room and then bundled me up and took me on the cold route down Market Street. We went from neon sign to neon sign until she found my parents or anyone who knew me and cared enough to claim me. On our walks, she held my hand tightly and told me I would be all right, and she attempted to assure me that no matter what, I would see her the next day.

On one particularly windy night, she shoved open the door to Clay and Jeff, the bar whose jukebox kept me company during my sleepless nights. The patrons looked surprised to see a five-year-old enter the bar, and my friend, still clutching me by the hand, asked, "Is Mr. or Mrs. Frances in here?"

I hung my head in shame, but then I heard, "I'll take her. I know who she is."

It was my uncle Nelse, an older man who wasn't actually my blood relation but was a good friend of the family. He always had a kind word for me and often welcomed me in his apartment a block away from where we lived.

The daycare worker let go of my hand and gave me a reassuring smile before leaving. Nelse helped me climb onto the barstool next to him and asked, "Want some chips, kid?"

I smiled behind tired eyes and nodded my head yes. I remembered this small kindness for the rest of my life.

The only time I recall feeling safe and cared for outside of

Wesley House was when our apartment manager, Ms. Margie, babysat my brother Bimbo and me while my mother and father went out to the bars. By the time I was five years old, we had moved out of the shotgun house into an apartment in the same neighborhood. Nights with Ms. Margie were unusual because not only did Bimbo and I have someone to look after us, but we also had food—warm, delicious food.

We gobbled hamburgers, fries, and ice cream from a neighborhood restaurant called Karalou's. There was no yelling or screaming, and there were no drunks to look after. After a peaceful evening, she put us down to rest in clean-smelling linen. Her apartment was always so much cleaner and warmer than ours.

One night in Ms. Margie's apartment, I was tucked in on the couch, lying on my side facing out to the rest of the room. I was not asleep yet, just enjoying the peace and quiet and my full belly, when a childlike figure appeared, kneeling beside the couch near my head. I entered into a trance-like state and could not move—not that I wanted to, as I was not afraid. Instead, I was strangely calm. The figure glowed, and sparkling light seemed to dance around it. It seemed to be praying for me in whispers of another language, but somehow I understood bits of what it was saying—that I was going to have a hard life but that it had come to give me strength.

A feeling of safety and calmness came over me as I lay there listening to whispers of reassurance that I would overcome the life ahead of me. This went on for some time, and I eventually fell asleep, though I have carried the memory with me throughout life.

Whenever I shared this story with others, I was sure they would not believe me. Even I wondered sometimes if I had been dreaming or if the streetlights were playing tricks on me.

But deep down, I knew that the figure was an angel and that it had come that night to give me strength. For life was not going to be anything different from what I had experienced so far. It would only get worse, and I was going to need the strength I received that night if I was going to survive to reach my calling.

\*

The apartment where we lived was near the slaughterhouse where the pigs and cows were killed and butchered. The stench carried for a three-block radius and was often so bad that we had to cover our mouths and noses with our clothes when walking to and from school. Directly across the street from our three-room apartment was a bar called Rosie's. Next to it was the Shelmar Follies, a triple-X movie theater, and a Goodwill, where we got all our clothes.

Next door to our apartment was Newrafth's Funeral Home. While animals were systematically slaughtered a few blocks away, my siblings and I watched, year after year, as the patrons of Rosie's bar slowly lived out most of their days at that bar and eventually became wards of the funeral home next door. At six years old, I played in the dirt outside and watched the bodies being rolled up the ramp and taken into the embalming room. On summer nights, my siblings and I lay together in the same room, several in the same bed or sharing blankets on the floor, with the curtains pulled back to catch a breeze. We would look out the window, knowing there were dead bodies just yards away from us, and my older brothers would scare me with ghost stories.

Meanwhile, the chaotic fights continued inside our apartment, sometimes lasting for days. The tension between my mother and father was constant, but when I was six years old, it reached a breaking point. They fought over everything, but what I remember most were their arguments over us kids. My mother in particular resented how my father treated me differently from my brothers. He would bring home treats and presents for me and get nothing for my brothers, and she thought he was overly harsh with the boys while letting me get away with everything.

Finally, one night, my father beat my brother Bimbo with a belt—though for what, I can't remember. Beatings like this weren't all that uncommon, but this time, the buckle hit Bimbo and gave him a black eye. My mother was outraged. It confirmed all of her fears and accusations, and the next morning, she, Bimbo, and the rest of my siblings were gone, leaving me alone with my father. Her anger at my father's mistreatment of Bimbo seemed greater than any love or concern she had for me. I felt like I was being punished for my own father loving me.

But rather than receiving more attention as the only child with my father, I was left alone more than ever. Now that there was no one at home to fight, my father joined the patrons at Rosie's bar every day. Hungry, I would stand by the door and stare at the bar, too afraid to cross the street alone to ask my father for food. And when he was home, I usually ended up being the caretaker, fetching him things at all hours when he was too drunk or too hung over to get off the couch. No one ever visited after my mother and siblings left. Not even Ms. Margie the landlady came to check on me.

One evening when my father finally staggered home, he was so drunk he could hardly stand. He made it to the front yard and stood on the steps screaming at the neighbors and yelling obscenities back across the street at the bar. As I watched, I remembered that adults often said to each other,

"Here, drink some coffee and sober up." So I ran as fast as my little legs would carry me to the kitchen to prepare what I thought would be the solution to his drunkenness.

I slid a chair across the floor to the sink, got a dirty cup from the drain, and hopped back off the chair to place several spoons of instant coffee into the cup, thinking more coffee would sober him up faster. I then climbed back onto the chair to run cold water into the cup. Instant coffee was all over the outside of the cup, but I was so proud of my accomplishment. Clutching the cup with both hands, I carried it through the apartment back outside to where my father was still screaming at the neighbors and the people standing outside the bar.

As I held the coffee up to him, I said, my voice quivering, "I made you coffee, Daddy." I stood barefoot and on my tiptoes on the cold concrete steps, and he took the cup from me. After one sip, he spat it out and threw the cup and all its contents in the front yard. I ran back inside the apartment to hide, knowing he was too far gone. All I could think was, *Why did he do that when I worked so hard to sober him up? Why won't he take care of me, the baby?*

When he finally made his way into the apartment, he passed out in his chair, and the next morning when I woke up, he was gone. I spent the whole day alone, waiting by the window again. The next day was the same, and the next and the next until I lost track of how many days had gone by. My father never came back, and there was no food anywhere in the house. I was, as so many times before, forgotten again.

I didn't know what to do as my body became weaker and weaker with hunger. Eventually, I started to feel sick, so I lay on the couch, facing the front door of the apartment, and waited, hoping someone would return for me. I felt like I had the flu; I was so exhausted and achy that I could hardly move.

But flu or no flu, I was definitely starving. All I could do was sleep and wait for someone to take care of me. Day turned into night, and night brought another day as I stared through the door and listened for anyone to return.

The ceilings were so high that the room seemed to swallow me. The front door was open to the hallway, allowing the cold air in. All I was wearing was a thin summer dress that my mother had left me in before she went away. In a haze, I stared at the steps that led to the second floor. By now, I couldn't get off the couch. I had given up on any family members ever returning when I heard scuffling on the front porch steps. Seconds later, a woman began to hurry up the stairs.

*No, it can't be*, I thought to myself. I thought I was imagining it, but it looked like my mother, heading to the landlady's apartment upstairs. "Mama!" I called out, and reached for her with my bony little arms. I began to cry, thinking she wasn't real. I had waited so long for someone to come and help me that I was at the point of delusion. Where had she been? She didn't exactly look like my mama; she was healthy, her face had makeup on it, and her hair was done up in curls.

For a moment, I thought for certain she was going to leave me again as she took two more steps up the stairs. But then she stopped, turned, and looked at me with shock on her face. "Mary?" she called tentatively, and I was sure it was my mother's voice. She walked slowly back down the steps toward me as if not believing what she was seeing. It seemed like months since I had last seen her. All I could think of was the memory of when she had put this thin dress on me the morning she left, and then my only thought was of food.

# CHAPTER THREE

# Kill the Kindness

The day my mother found me and saved my life was the day I first met Tucker. Tucker was a skinny little man who was balding and not much to look at, but my mother loved him and had been with him ever since she left me with my father. Tucker had my mother's approval because he knew how to hold a job and had served in the military, and he quickly gained my approval because he always answered my questions about life, no matter how ridiculous. Without fail, he would stuff his hands in his pockets, look at the floor, and answer, "Well, Mary Lou, it's like this," and go on to answer whatever silly question I had. He told me stories and shared his wisdom, and I gobbled up every word.

It didn't take long to recover from starvation once I was with my mother and Tucker. My very first breakfast with them included milk, cereal, and bananas. We rarely had luxuries like fruit and milk, and I was in heaven consuming them. I was also excited to be reunited with my brother Bimbo, whom I was closer to than any of my siblings since we were the two youngest. Our mother often said Bimbo was mildly retarded, but I knew even in my young heart that it was our environment that had slowed him down.

On my first day in my new home in Old Louisville, the sun shone through the windows of our apartment, and everything seemed clean, bright, and warm. Laughter filled the room—something I had not heard for what seemed an eternity. My mother had a smile on her face and seemed to be a whole new person as she watched Tucker wrestle and play with us.

Bimbo was different too; he and my mother always used to make snide remarks about me and leave me out of things because of the way my father favored me. But now with Tucker, Bimbo began to feel equally loved, and all the competition and rivalry quickly melted away. I had missed his presence during our time apart and was relieved to have my Bim back.

For a while, life was blessed. Our new apartment was large enough that Bimbo and I each had our own room with our own bed—a far cry from the floor we had slept on in the apartment my father had abandoned me in. Although my mother and Tucker continued to drink, at least some of the violence had stopped, and there was food daily for my brother and me.

After missing more than a month of school, I reentered the first grade, but I spent most of my first day crying because I was afraid my mother wouldn't return for me at the end of the day. I cried off and on the entire day until I couldn't breathe. The following day, I was anxious and worried, but then, day after day, Mama would pick us up, and I began to trust that she would come back for me.

Unfortunately, this peace didn't last long. Mama soon began to abuse Tucker both physically and verbally. Drunk or sober, she often punched him in the chest for no reason, just because she could. In all the times I witnessed her mistreating him, I never once saw Tucker put his hands on her. But this was only a hint of the abuse to come, albeit from another source.

On our first Thanksgiving together, Mama wanted to make it a day to remember. By then, she had pieced together full sets of furniture and pretty decorations to fill our apartment, and she spent the whole morning preparing a Thanksgiving meal with all the fixings. The smell of the turkey in the oven and the sound of water boiling and knives chopping made our little place feel like home. While the turkey finished, we went out to visit relatives. Little did we know that on that same day, my father and older brothers had found out where we lived and decided to pay us a visit.

We came home to an apartment destroyed from one end to the other. Furniture was turned over, every dish in the kitchen was broken, and cigarette butts were smashed into our turkey. The rest of the food was slung all over the kitchen. Gravy dripped from the ceiling and mashed potatoes from the walls; smashed vegetables covered the floor. I began to cry, knowing my new life had been too good to be true.

Mama and Tucker cleaned up the ruined food and broken furniture, and we had a small spaghetti dinner sitting on the couch, which was thankfully still intact. Just as Bimbo and I were about to be shooed off to bed, the thundering of heavy footsteps filled the hallway outside our door. Tucker had barely stood up when the door was suddenly kicked in from the outside. There stood my father and three of my brothers, drunk and with a murderous gleam in their eyes.

My father ordered my older brothers to beat Tucker. My brothers, all grown and muscular, overpowered skinny, balding Tucker in an instant and beat him until his eyeball was lying out on his cheek. Bimbo and I screamed, and Mama cursed and wailed, helpless to intervene. We had seen fights before, but nothing as brutal as what poor Tucker was taking from the three of them all at once. I feared he would die before the ambulance came to take him away. Eventually, they stopped, leaving Tucker semiconscious and lying in a pool of blood.

\*

Thankfully, Tucker survived, with both eyes and all his limbs intact. Still, my father and brothers succeeded in driving us from our haven in Old Louisville. Soon we were back to the neighborhood of Butchertown, where I had lived all my life. Our new house was half a block away from Wesley House, the community center that had always brought me such joy. By now, I was seven years old and in the second grade at Lincoln Elementary. Since I lived next to Wesley House and was old enough to walk home by myself, there was no more shame waiting for parents who never came to pick me up.

Being back in Butchertown seemed to break the happy spell my mother had been under in the few months after she rescued me from my father's apartment. Her old feelings about me returned—feelings of resentment over the way my father had favored me and her own guilt over allowing her other children to be sold. She barely looked at me and some days didn't even respond when I tried to talk to her. Even at that young age, I began to really understand the depth of my mother's resentment toward me, and familiar feelings of desperation and loneliness quickly replaced any new sense of security Tucker had brought into my life.

Still, the more my mother ignored me, the more I wanted her. As my mother continued to fail me, I found the love I craved in a prostitute named Regina, whom my brother Richard was dating. Richard hadn't been involved in Tucker's beating because he was still in prison for murder. Regina had been with Richard for years, and so my mother tolerated her coming and going whenever she stopped by to ask how Richard was doing. Since my mother wanted very little to do with her, Regina instead joined me in the kitchen while I played my records, and she would talk to me for what felt like hours of bliss.

In addition to prostitution, Regina worked as a "go-go dancer" (a stripper, in today's terminology). She would show me her stage costumes, made of fringe, tassels, and sequins, and I thought they were the most beautiful clothes I'd ever seen. She also told me stories about how she danced nude. "If the top comes off, Mary, so do the bottoms," she said as she showed me how the costumes snapped on and off.

As I played my forty-fives, she would pull me off my chair and dance with me, taking me by the hand and teaching me how to sway my hips. She showed me "The Shimmy" and "The Big Bee," which required us to shake our hips as fast as we could. I would dance alongside her, exerting so much energy and laughter that I finally fell to the floor from exhaustion.

Regina gave me her undivided attention and answered all my questions, something that I craved. I didn't know what a harlot or a go-go dancer was; I just knew I wanted to be loved, and Regina loved everyone. She hugged me and told me things I shouldn't have heard about the nude bar where she worked. She let me know that I was worthy to be loved even when I didn't think I was important. She also told me about my brother in prison and how she loved him and how amazing he was.

I looked forward to Richard getting out of prison because he had also always shown me love when our mother took me along with her to visit him in prison. I'll never forget how scared I was when the iron gates slammed behind me, and as young as I was, I still recognized the desperation in the eyes of the prisoners whenever we visited.

Every time after one of these joyful visits with Regina, I would cry myself to sleep. One time my mother caught me doing so and snapped, "What the hell is wrong with you?"

"I want Regina to come back," I sniffed.

"That whore? You've gotta be kidding me."

Anger burned inside me whenever I heard her say such ugly things because I knew there was no love to be found outside of Regina. Music had brought us together, and it wouldn't be the last time music would help fill the void in my young life.

*

Down the block from our house on Franklin Street stood two houses where a large black family lived—brothers, sisters, aunts, uncles, and cousins all crammed in together. The family intrigued and fascinated me as I sat playing in the dirt with bare feet, my dirty hair strung across my face. It was the spring of 1968, and I was seven years old. Life had shown me nothing but violence, alcoholism, and sex, and I was becoming depressed even at a young age. I needed to feel something besides the unworthiness I had experienced.

I heard the sounds of Motown for the first time as our neighbors' live band played every evening. It was the best music I had ever heard, better than my records or the jukebox in Clay and Jeff, and I would sit on the curb scribbling in the dirt while my stomach rumbled at the smell of food cooking on charcoal.

All the women sat in the front yard straightening one another's hair with an iron comb. They laid the comb on a hot plate until it glowed red and then carefully placed the hot iron almost to their scalps before they pulled it out to produce straight hair or curls. I could smell the lard that they had slathered in their hair whenever the hot iron touched it.

Laughter was everywhere, and at times there were fifty or more people gathered, all of them related in some way. They drank alcohol but didn't fight like my family, as the matriarch grandmother wouldn't stand for any behavior that quenched the spirit of happiness. I watched as everyone got up to dance to the sound of their band playing soul music and the blues. It was another world, so strange and yet so beautiful.

I'll never forget the nights when one of the children would tug on my hand to invite me into their slice of heaven. A feeling of warmth and acceptance would come over me like a summer breeze. The celebration of family was in the air for the simple reason of being alive and together. For the first time, I could be something other than what I was known to be—that poor, skinny little white girl who wandered the streets, seeming not to belong to anyone or anything.

It was an awesome feeling to be among them. I shook my hips as Regina had taught me and did "The Jerk," another popular dance in the 1960s. I felt safe and a part of something real. But then darkness would come upon us and the grandmother would tell me to make my way home, and I would be forced to return to the chaos that was my real life. Still, this family taught me that true familial love existed, and the desire for it burned in my heart, leading me to look for it even in the darkest of places.

# CHAPTER FOUR

# Summer in the Clarksdale Projects

In the summer of 1968, Mama and Tucker moved us just blocks away from Butchertown into government housing called the Clarksdale Projects. The projects consisted of block upon block of identical red brick buildings, where no grass grew or flowers bloomed within the courtyards. Several dumpsters stood in the alleys between each building. The smell of garbage dominated the streets, and the air became thick with flies when it was hot outside.

In the summertime, families sat out in their small pieces of yard in the ninety-degree heat to escape the even more unbearable heat of the concrete walls inside. Barefoot children with hungry bellies played marbles in the dirt to pass the time. The music of Motown rang throughout the courtyards—the only welcoming sound in this whole place. Although it was just blocks away from Wesley House, where I had had so many good memories, the year I lived in this neighborhood marked a period of intense loneliness and a break in innocence that would usher me down the darkest of paths.

Although the neighborhood was new, the drunken nights

inside my home continued just the same. I was seven years old now, but the screaming and fighting still frightened me, so I spent many nights hiding in my bedroom, praying that none of the adults would come to my room to use my bed for sex. I spent hours alone in the dark with no one to talk to and nothing to do to pass the time except listen to the reveling below.

The only times I did have company were when my mother's best friend brought her seventeen-year-old daughter over to our house. The daughter used to babysit me often, and so at first, it was a relief to have a familiar presence in the room. However, one night, what should have been a safe space became worse than the brawling outside. That night, when the screaming started, she took my hand, led me to the bedroom, and closed the door behind us. She pulled me onto the bed with her and held me tight—at first I thought to comfort me. But then her hand slid beneath my clothes.

I froze, scared and unsure of what was happening, as she fondled me until she was satisfied. On some level, I knew what was happening was wrong, but what could I do? Every adult who I would have gone to was long past the point of drunkenness, and even if I hadn't been too ashamed and scared to speak, I wasn't sure I would have the words to explain what had happened.

This abuse went on for some time. As if I didn't have enough reason to dread the parties, I now had to wait anxiously every day wondering if my abuser would come to haunt me that night. It didn't matter if I tried to stay out of the bed or pretended to be asleep; if she wanted my company, she would have it. Although my grades were terrible, I was actually looking forward to the school year starting because I wondered if school might distract her away from me.

But relief didn't come until she finally found a boyfriend. She became pregnant in fairly short order, and only then did she leave me alone. The baby she had was the only beauty in that house, and I loved her for coming along because she marked the end of my abuse.

My mother never knew that any of this had gone on. In fact, my family and my abuser's family continued to be close friends and spent many summer evenings together. One such evening, our families went to the park for a picnic. We had a huge spread, complete with meat, fruit, and of course generous amounts of alcohol. Everyone got drunk pretty quickly as they pounded back beer after beer to keep cool. Most of them passed out, and a few others went wandering through the park while I attempted to grill the hot dogs.

I dumped the old charcoal on the ground thinking it had gone out. Then I took the charcoal fluid, sprinkled it on the grill, and lit matches to ignite the new charcoal. As the grill began to smoke, I walked over to grab the hot dogs and accidentally stepped on one of the old charcoals I'd dumped on the ground. It turned out that the old charcoal was still hot—and I immediately knew exactly how hot, because I stepped on it with bare feet. I shrieked and began to dance around, screaming at the top of my lungs. Everywhere I stepped, there was another hot coal.

My mother's best friend was sprawled out on a blanket on the ground, and she was the only one to wake up immediately at my screams. She seized me and dragged me away from the hot coals, and then plunged both of my feet into a tub of ice along with the watermelon and beer. My brothers carried the tub and me (my feet still submerged in the ice water) and placed me in the back seat of the car. When we got home, they carried me inside, and I slept with my feet in the tub all night.

The next day, the bottoms of my feet were completely blistered, and I was unable to walk for the rest of the summer. From the window, I watched the other children playing, and a deep loneliness set in as I sat isolated in the chaos of my house. Once the blisters finally popped, I took to walking on my heels to go outside and play, which did nothing to increase my popularity, as the other kids already made fun of me due to my family's reputation. I was never taken to the doctor for my burns.

Although I was only seven years old, a deep and abiding anger had settled in the middle of my chest, an anger that I could neither help nor explain. I hated everything around me except my best friend, Allen, who was the one sane part of my life. Allen was a nerdy white boy with black-frame glasses who didn't believe in God and cursed every other word. I was forever trying to convince him that God was real because I was afraid God would strike him down for some of his beliefs. However, I admired and cared very much for Allen because he never let anything concern or scare him. He protected me whenever the other girls made fun of my clothes and the fact that I hung around a boy.

Allen and I used to walk or ride our bikes for miles to get to the park, where we caught minnows and turtles to take home as pets. When the heat was unbearable, we walked to the Ohio River, and unattended by adults, we jumped off the docks and swam in the dangerous currents. Although we each had other friends, Allen was where my innocence was safe, and when all the girls were doing girly things, Allen and I spent our time studying the NASA space program and mail-ordering models of the Apollo spacecraft that we would build and glue together.

But not even Allen could shield me from my next abuser, who made his move the summer I turned eight years old. He was sixty years old and claimed to be my mother's cousin, and whenever he visited our house, he tried to impress everyone with his diamonds and gold. He owned a car lot and a mansion on the river in Indiana. This wealthy man took an interest in me and started to buy me clothes and toys whenever he came around.

It wouldn't be long before I learned to manipulate him for money, and without any pressure, he would take me out for ice cream and shopping and would buy me whatever I wanted. He even took Allen and me on camping trips in his RV and joy rides in a two-man plane. He treated me special, and I felt as if I was better than the other children, though all the while he was grooming me for one particular night.

Because this man was so wealthy, my mother allowed him to spend all this time alone with me without comment. In fact, whenever he took me on trips to Bernheim Forest, he always gave her money before we left. It was no different on this last camping trip, when, after several months of gifts and treats, he finally made his move.

This particular time, it was just the two of us going in his RV overnight. We roasted hot dogs and marshmallows, and once I had stuffed myself full, I went into the RV and fell asleep in the top bunk of the bed. Sometime deep in the night, I was awakened by his presence standing over me on the bunk. His hand was down my panties, and he was bent over me trying to kiss me.

I sat bolt upright and pulled away from him, screaming, "Get off of me!"

He did so immediately. Once he saw I was not going to let him do what he wanted, he backed away and left me alone. Still shocked and wanting to get as far away from him as possible, I climbed down from the bunk and fled to the front seat of the cab.

He followed me and sat in the driver's seat. "It's okay, Mary. Nothing happened. I'll give you five dollars if you don't tell your mom about this."

"I don't want your money," I spat. "Go away and leave me alone."

Then I turned my back to him and scooted my body as far away from him as I could while cramped in the front seat. For most of the night, I sat there with my arms and legs folded tight, pouting in the dark and refusing to speak. I couldn't believe that I had been fooled into thinking I was special. While staring out the window, I tried to focus on the sounds of crickets and frogs, and eventually, I fell asleep there in the front seat.

The next day, neither of us mentioned anything about the incident. Instead, he dropped me off at home, and I never told a soul about what had happened. It was just too ugly and embarrassing to talk about. For the rest of the summer, I took baths at least four times a day to try to feel clean again, but nothing seemed to help.

Meanwhile, my body was starting to come down with its worst sickness since my father had left me to starve in our apartment in Butchertown. After a few days of aching, swelling, and fever, I was admitted to the hospital with scarlet fever. For more than a month, I was left there, weak, medicated, and isolated 24/7. Once my family dropped me off, they didn't come back even once to visit or check on me. I had no television, radio, or books to help the hours pass as I sat miserable and alone in that hospital room.

After a week of this mind-numbing loneliness, my mother's cousin came to visit, looking as guilty and uncomfortable as he had the morning after the incident in the RV. However, in his hands was a TV, and my eyes fixed on it as he entered the room. My thoughts warred within me; I loathed the gift giver and knew it was probably a bribe to keep me quiet about his sins, but I knew that TV would improve hospital life considerably. He set it up right next to me, and I tried to say as little as possible until he got the hint and left.

Another week went by, and I tried not to think about him as I watched hour after hour of TV. But then, after that glorious week, the TV broke.

I stared and stared at the broken TV, and the longer I stared, the angrier I became. Why had no one come to visit me except this man? How was he even allowed to come see me? And how dare he continue to bring me expensive gifts as if everything about what he had done was okay?

Then he came—again. I was in a foul mood, and the sight of him only stirred the anger that had been building the last few weeks.

"How are you doing?" he asked. "Are you any better?"

My only response was, "Take your damn broken TV and get it out of my room."

"It broke? I can get you another—"

"No! I want you to leave!"

"It's really no prob—"

He didn't get to finish because I picked up the television and threw it on the floor at his feet. It shattered into a dozen pieces, and the nurse came rushing into the room to see what was going on.

"Get out! I want him out!" I yelled.

He scrambled to pick up the pieces of the TV and hurried out the door with it.

"And don't come back!" I screamed after him.

Bewildered, the nurse asked, "What was that all about?"

"Nothing," I said. I was too ashamed to explain. No one had come to see me but the one person who I thought was a nice man, but even he turned out to be like all the others who had hurt me.

By the time I finally got out of the hospital, school had already started, and I had missed the first few weeks. As if I weren't lost and behind already. And to make matters worse, Allen's family had moved away, and I was left alone again to face the bullies and my own loneliness and isolation.

However, I was soon blessed with a new friend named Sally. Unlike the other girls I had had so much trouble with, she was quiet and shy, and she didn't judge me. We started walking to and from school together and then spent all day at school keeping each other company. She was a gentle and calming presence in the middle of my day, providing an escape from the anger and shouting at home.

But then one day our friendship was cut tragically short. As school was ending for the day, Sally was standing to empty her desk. Another child had come behind her to get to the pencil sharpener and moved Sally's chair to get through, and when Sally went to sit back down, she missed the chair and fell to the floor, hitting her head on the wall.

The rest of the class laughed as our teacher called us to attention. Sally gathered herself together and went to the back of the room to retrieve her coat from the closet. Before she could make it back to her desk, she began to vomit.

Our teacher sent her to the office to lie down, and her younger sister waited for her to feel well enough to take the walk home. Sally's mother worked and was not aware that she had injured herself that day in school or had walked home in her condition. When her mother came home, she assumed that Sally just had a stomach bug when she found her daughter lying down and vomiting. Thankfully, Sally's sister told their mother what had happened, and they rushed Sally to the hospital.

But it was too late.

The next morning, I headed over to Sally's apartment across the alley to walk with her to school. A neighbor stopped me along the way and hung her head out the window to tell me that Sally had died the night before from a head injury.

I screamed and ran back to my house. Sobbing, I leaned on our doorbell and shrieked, "Mama!"

Although probably still hung over, my mother stuck her head out the window, and looking startled, she asked, "What's wrong, Mary?"

"Mama, Sally is gone. Iris said she died last night."

When she was drunk and angry, my mother's face became taut and pale, so I always knew when it was time to run. But there was another side to my mother, buried down deep—one that was kind and compassionate and had a very wise view of the world. So when my mother heard what had happened to my gentle friend, her features suddenly softened, and she said, "Oh no, Mary, I am so sorry."

I hung on the door in tears and couldn't believe it. After several minutes of grief, anger suddenly started to flood in. I was going to beat up the child who had pulled Sally's chair out of her reach. I couldn't wait to get to school to blame the little girl and accuse her of killing Sally in front of everyone else in our class.

I marched to school, full of righteous anger, and went directly to the lunchroom, where all the children were eating breakfast.

As soon as I spotted the girl, I screamed, "You killed her! You killed my best friend!"

Everyone in the lunchroom stopped talking to look at us. The other girl looked shocked and frightened, and had only tears in response to my hateful accusation.

Deep down, I knew she had only moved the chair to sharpen her pencil. She hadn't tried to hurt Sally on purpose. But I had such rage and spite in my own heart that I never considered her feelings, as she was distraught and guilt-ridden already.

My heart was broken for Sally. Each morning I went into the classroom and sat next to the desk where my best friend had sat, and I often forgot and thought she would walk through the door after me. Our school went to the funeral services that week, and I remember I was upset that her braids were different from how she usually wore them as she lay in her little coffin.

The children in our class never received any counseling for our loss. We returned to school and went back to doing what we normally did. I grieved for my friend and for my own loss, and I was reminded daily of my lonely life as I sat staring at her empty desk.

# CHAPTER FIVE

# Freedom

Things at home never got better. My mother eventually drove Tucker away, so I was left alone with her pain and her drunken, manic episodes. With each incident, her behavior became even more destructive. I would hide in my room until I heard her call my name in an intoxicated stupor to come downstairs when she needed someone to talk to. She always sat at the window looking out at nothing, sipping her coffee to sober up. Everyone who had helped her get drunk would leave the house to get away from her, but I had nowhere to go and was too young to run.

Even if it was three o'clock in the morning and I had school the next morning, I knew that if I didn't answer her calls, everything would be worse because she would feel I was rejecting her. It was the same conversation every time, and it always started with her, tears streaming from her eyes, asking me, "Do you love me, Mary?"

"Yes, Mama, I love you," I said. I would repeat this over and over for hours, hurt and exhausted and bewildered that I had to convince her that I loved her.

"I am a stupid b———," she would sob, pounding her chest with her open hands.

"No, you're not, Mama! Please don't say things like that about yourself."

"He sold my babies away," she moaned. "I hate him, and it's all my fault I let him sell them."

Then she cried for the children she could not feed. She told me stories about my father going back to the people he had sold my siblings to and asking for more money to feed the rest of us. Sometimes they took pity on him, but inevitably, he would keep the money for himself while we continued to starve.

Meanwhile, when she became pregnant with me, my mother took a job for a woman named Mary doing her ironing and housekeeping. It was long, backbreaking work. My mother spent all day dusting and polishing Mary's fine china and picking up after her prize show dogs while our own home remained filthy and empty. My mother tried so hard to impress that woman by doing a good job and trying to act more sophisticated than she was. But at the end of the day, all she went home with were a few dollars and a pot of soup because Mary knew our family needed food more than anything.

In fact, Mary had helped my parents find buyers for some of their children. One brother had gone to the dog breeder who sold Mary her Chihuahuas. A sister went to one of Mary's acquaintances when they heard she was starving under my parents' care. By the time I came along, I think my father's guilt over taking money and creating lies and scandal got the better of him, and he insisted on keeping me—something my mother came to resent bitterly. Sometimes during these drunken storytelling episodes, she would start to scream at me out of nowhere and call me by my father's name. "You're just like your daddy!" she would say as she punched me in the chest. "You're just like that damn Johnny boo and nothing like the rest of us."

That part was true at least. I wasn't and didn't want to be like any of my relatives. They stole from one another, beat each other, and had no respect for themselves or anyone else. It was a heavy load of shame to carry. I was depressed and anxious for everything, always afraid something bad would happen. The worst part was that the next day, when she had sobered up, my mother acted as though nothing had happened the night before, while I went to school exhausted.

Every day as I walked home from school, I wished and hoped that I would find my mother sober—if she was home at all. Even before climbing the porch steps, I knew what I was heading into based on the smells and sounds that came through the front door. On a really good day, I might smell dinner cooking. But if all was quiet, I knew the house was empty and there would be food stamps on the kitchen counter so I could go to the store and then prepare my own meals, even as young as eight years old.

Afterward, I went next door to watch television with a friend, all the while waiting and listening for my mother to return. As soon as I heard her coming through the courtyard screaming obscenities, I hurried home so she wouldn't show up at my friend's house looking for me. Then, depending on how drunk she was, the cycle would begin again.

*Just hide, Mary,* I thought to myself. *Someday the pain is going to end, someday.*

\*

With Sally out of my life, I became lonely and even more depressed. I tried very hard to do well in school, but after years of being up all night either hiding from or caring for drunks, it was as if my brain couldn't process the complicated things my teachers were trying to tell me.

Feeling lost and ashamed, I took my homework over to my cousin Dolores, the one with polio, who was now a young woman in her teens living with her grandmother across the alley from us in the housing projects. Dolores knew how much my mother left me home alone, so she welcomed me with open arms and spent hours trying to teach me fifth-grade math. Over and over, she patiently explained simple division, but there was no getting through to me.

As we worked, we drank coffee—something I thought was good and healthy since it quenched my hunger and sobered up the drunks. I drank so much that I became addicted to it; I had five or more cups a day and even had a cup before school in the mornings.

Dolores took every opportunity to watch over me and feed me, and many times my only meal of the day would be under Dolores's watch. She couldn't understand how any mother could receive aid from the state and not see to it that her children were fed. One day in a fit of righteous anger, she took me to my father's house, not far from where we lived in the projects. By then, he had taken up with another woman and her children, none of whom had any love for me. I knew it was useless to go to them because my father always kept a long chain and padlock around the refrigerator and food pantry, and he unlocked them only at mealtimes so my stepsisters could cook for him.

But on this day, Dolores marched us over to his house and stood as tall as her polio would allow her. "Your child is hungry," she said as I stood a few steps behind her on his front porch. "She hasn't eaten all day, and this keeps happening day in and day out. What are you going to do about it?"

My father waved her off as he took a drag from his cigarette. "Take her a—— to Emma. She should be feeding her."

Dolores was indignant, but there was no persuading him. Instead, she took me down the street to Karalou's restaurant. As we sat across from each other, I bounced my legs against the booth, feeling like I had won a trip to the carnival. When our food came, I devoured my cheeseburger and shoved food in my mouth like it was my last meal. I swallowed each bite before chewing properly and left ketchup and mayonnaise smeared across my face as I moved on to my fries. Shocked, Dolores watched me practically lick my plate clean and then finish off her grilled cheese.

Life went on like this for years. I survived by tagging along behind my cousin and found freedom from my mother by staying with Dolores every chance I got. But Dolores couldn't be with me at school, and so I drifted along quietly, always feeling like the dumbest and poorest kid in class.

This all changed when a girl named Angie befriended me when I was fourteen years old. I hadn't had a female friend around my age since Sally's death. I wasn't sure why Angie wanted to be my friend. She was very popular and a leader; I was teased and haunted by my family's poor reputation. Her nails were manicured and her hair was thick and long; I wore whatever hand-me-downs were given to me. She was a healthy weight; I was ragged, frail, and thin. While my brothers sat in jail and my mother ignored me, Angie's mother bought cute clothes, jewelry, and toys for Angie and her siblings. She was everything the boys wanted; there was so much about me that made no boy want to talk to me.

So when Angie wanted to be my friend and take the lead all the time, I was all for it because I couldn't think for myself. I desired to be just like Angie because I never knew who I was. I observed her and the love she had in her life without jealousy because I knew I was something just because I was her friend.

I found myself staying overnight with Angie several nights a week to escape my mother's drunken madness. Eventually, it got to where I was at her house or my cousin's house more than my own. Although they welcomed me unconditionally, when there was no one in the kitchen and no one was watching, I would steal food in fits of self-preservation. In a hurry so no one would catch me, I grabbed food or ate straight out of Angie's mother's pots. The shame I carried in the back of my mind must have shown on my face even when we were hanging out with Angie's big group of friends. While all the other girls were worried about boys, I was worried about where I'd get my next meal.

My mother never knew or was concerned if I was gone for days. I needed freedom away from my mother, and my friend's mother treated me like one of her own. Angie and I had both been raised in Butchertown, and like everyone else, Angie's mother knew I was unwanted.

Angie's family lived next door to a biker gang, and when we became friends, I began to take the school bus home with her. Little did I know that this decision would affect my life for the next thirty-five years.

# CHAPTER SIX

# Two Ice-Cream Seasons

Pimps and perpetrators come in many forms. Some have families, and some look like businessmen; but the one who pursued me was a member of the Vagrants biker gang who was thirteen years older than I was. At the time we met, he had several women in prostitution, who handed over their money while he was busy planning my future as he watched me grow up next door at my best friend's house.

He stood more than six feet tall beside my eighty-pound body. He was handsome and had an air about himself that impressed most people. He was a hustler, and those who knew him would say even today that he is a legend. Dirty Dan was what the Vagrant bikers called him, but I called him Dirty—not because of his hygiene, but because of the terrible things he did to me and expected me to do for him.

I was fifteen years old when I first met him standing at the ice cream truck that drove through our neighborhood every summer. The Vagrants had bought the house next door to Angie's, and the two-story red brick building served both as meeting space and living quarters for many of the men in the gang. Since I stayed at Angie's house more than my own at this point, I had grown accustomed to the roar of the Harley

Davidson motorcycles that lined the street and the strange men and women who went in and out of the clubhouse at all hours.

Whenever Dirty Dan bought the neighborhood children ice cream, he would give everyone else popsicles but tell me I could have whatever I wanted. I had never been singled out like this before (at least not for anything good). While boys my own age never even looked at me, the neighborhood legend Dirty Dan seemed to think I was special, and that was enough to make my neglected heart soar.

From the safety of Angie's second-story bedroom, she and I watched everything that went on in the yard of the Vagrants' clubhouse. Most prominent were the pit bulls they kept chained up outside year-round. Besides their bikes, these dogs were the Vagrants' most prized possessions, although they used them for sport and forced them to fight one another while their owners bet on the outcomes.

The men themselves dressed in leather, head to toe, and the full-fledged members proudly wore patches on the back of their vests. They referred to outsiders as "citizens," as if the Vagrants lived separate from and above the society around them, and they put their initiates, or probates, through a lengthy probationary period before they were rewarded with their member patches.

Although only men could officially be in the club, there were just as many, if not more, women who partied with them day and night. Many of the bikers had more than one woman (whom they called "ol' ladies") under their control, and Angie and I often overheard them talking about buying or trading these women. At times, the men gave the women to each other as gifts or to pay off debts. The value of the ol' ladies wasn't in their love and companionship; rather, it was in how much money they could bring their ol' men through stripping and prostitution (which they called "turning tricks").

The Vagrants were aware that I was an unwanted child who had no safe place but my friend's house to live. They saw me as potential material and were waiting for me to get old enough to become an asset to the club. My lack of guidance and parental protection was to their advantage. At that age, I didn't notice them watching me as I stepped off the school bus and as I walked down the sidewalk toward my friend's house. They were just part of the scenery—although admittedly an interesting part.

Although I was aware of their lifestyle and how dangerous they were, and was often warned by my friend's mother not to talk to them, I was much too young to understand or believe that I was being set up to become an ol' lady. Those women held a sort of glamour for Angie and me as we leaned across the fence to talk to them, even as some sported black eyes and talked about being "put out" or passed around for sex among the men. From Angie's bedroom, we could see beyond the clubhouse's balcony into the bedrooms since there were no curtains. Being curious teenagers, we watched and witnessed far more than our minds could comprehend.

On Tuesdays, the Vagrants held "church," which was meeting night for all the men in the club. Motorcycles would roar down the street and fill up every inch of curb, and it seemed as if leather and beer cans spilled from every opening of the house. First, they had a private meeting where they paid dues, planned for events, and voted for club offices. Then the party began.

Music and laughter and their drunken spirit flowed through my friend's house in the summer months. Those nights became all the louder when "out-of-towners" descended on the neighborhood, coming from all directions around the country. Their patches reading "Nashville" or "Atlanta" or other far-flung cities made the Vagrants and their business feel larger than life to our insular neighborhood.

No matter where they were from, all the Vagrants looked like Dirty Dan—long, stringy hair and beards, leather from head to foot, boots, tattoos, and an air of danger. Most of them had returned from the Vietnam War and brought back with them hatred and disrespect for society, creating this subculture of brotherhood. They were loyal and bound by a sick sort of love among themselves. They often greeted one another with a kiss while they treated their women and dogs as property. When I knew them in the 1970s, the Vagrants were powerful, dangerous, and a step ahead of the law. They were also feared, respected, and idolized by our community, and no one from the world outside dared tread on their turf.

When Angie and I did interact with the men, they would leer at us as we walked past the clubhouse and call us "candy little girl." The president of the club would then scream at them, reminding them that we were underage. As scary as they were, I wasn't used to such attention, and bad or good, it was something for which I was willing to sell my soul. As I tagged behind my pretty and popular friend, the entire neighborhood knew I was the poor little white-trash girl who carried her whole wardrobe in a brown paper bag. I was an easy target for men like this to prey upon.

But back then, I didn't think of Dirty Dan as a predator. Unlike the other men, Dirty Dan didn't catcall us; he was just the man who bought me ice cream—and special ice cream at that.

One hot summer day, Dirty Dan bought everyone ice cream as usual, but he got me an expensive milkshake. While I gorged it like the starving child I was, Dirty leaned against the truck next to me and said, "Mary, I have to go away for a little while, but I'll be back for you in two ice-cream seasons."

I barely looked up from my milkshake but thought, *What in the world is an ice-cream season?*

When he saw my look of confusion, he continued, "When I get back, I'm gonna marry you and make you a star. I'll put your name in lights, baby."

I laughed nervously. "Okay, Dan." I gave it no more thought and left him by the ice cream truck so I could brag to the other children about my special treat.

Later I found out that he had to serve time in the Florida State Penitentiary beginning that summer. I didn't think I would ever see him again, much less become his ol' lady. In fact, I barely ever thought of Dirty Dan, especially when I found love that—if the Vagrants had known about it—would have cost me my life.

*

While Dan was away in prison, I fell in love with a boy from another race. Although I had grown up around black people all my life and didn't think anything of it, the 1970s were a time of racial revolution and hate. Many still believed that inter-racial love was something that should be punished, and the rest turned their heads while interracial couples were battered or shunned from society.

His name was Ray, and we met when he was seventeen and I was fifteen. We became best friends, and he gave me the love and attention I desperately needed. The community had long ago labeled me "white trash," and this new development did nothing to help ward off the bullies. I didn't see any problem with our relationship though. The one value my mother had taught me was not to hate people because they were different. It was the one thing my mother had instilled in me that made sense.

I remembered one day in our kitchen when she was sober, my brother was making racial remarks as he discussed the race riots going on around us. After one last slur, my mother had had enough and slammed a pot down on the counter. She glared at my brother and shouted, "What would you do if you got to heaven and God was black?"

You could hear a pin drop. Her outburst didn't stop the rioting and gang fights in the streets, but it impacted me at an early age and helped me to look at others for who they were, not for their skin color.

So I grew to love that seventeen-year-old boy who accepted me. Besides our deep love for one another, we had at least one thing in common: We were both poor. We escaped the stressors of our world through joint after joint of the finest marijuana the 1970s had to offer, and if felt as if no one could touch us when we were together. Even in the heat of arguments, we never disrespected one another with the racial remarks that were so common around us.

It was a love like no other, and neither of us saw beyond that. We each suffered for the other's love, but no matter how many threats or insults I endured from friends and family alike, they couldn't purge the love I had for him.

But not even teenagers in love can overcome the force of law. The night we were separated forever was no different from any other. My mother couldn't have cared less where I was, so I was content to stay the night with my love at his house. Feeling secure in his arms, I snuggled with him in his bed, both of us undressed and half asleep after another blissful evening together.

But that peace and that feeling of safety were not mine to keep. Suddenly, the bedroom door was kicked open, and it boomed spectacularly as the frame's usual warping and swelling was overcome by the force of the blow. Ray and I shot up in the bed as the overhead light flooded the previously pitch-black room and what seemed to be a hundred white police officers barreled inside.

Ray threw his arm in front of me while I scrunched behind him for protection. In seconds, they noticed the different color of our skin, and they all started screaming for us to get out of the bed.

"Get out of here!" Ray yelled, looking ready to jump out of bed and fight for me. "This is my girl. We're not doing anything wrong!"

It turned out Ray's brother had been seeing a girl who was a lot younger than he was, and her mother had called the police when the girl hadn't come home that night. They had come to the apartment looking for her, but instead they found Ray and me undressed and asleep in his bed.

It was 1975, but up until 1967, interracial marriage had been illegal in Kentucky. However, the officers in the room with us didn't seem to care much about what the Supreme Court had said just eight years before, because they ordered us to get dressed and come with them, in spite of Ray's insistence that we were innocent. Then they backed out of the room with looks of disgust on their faces and stood right outside the door, calling us racial names and discussing us as if we were animals.

Once the police were out of the room, I clutched the sheet to my breast and was unable to speak from shock. It was mortifying enough to be barged in on naked with my boyfriend, but by police officers of all people? My lifelong fear of authority, planted deep in my heart by seeing my brothers behind bars all my life, came rising to the surface, and I was finding it hard to breathe. What had we done wrong? What was going to happen to us?

Seeing my panic, Ray grabbed me by the shoulders. "Mary," he said.

For a moment, I couldn't focus on him because I couldn't tune out the racial slurs being hurled around outside our door.

"Mary, look at me."

I made myself look into his eyes.

"It's going to be okay. I love you."

"I love you too," I said as a tear slid down my face.

An officer banged on the door. "Hurry up and get dressed," he barked.

"Give us a minute," Ray hollered.

Everything was moving in slow motion. I felt as if my mind had left my body as I rose, shaking, and pulled on my clothes, missing arm and leg holes several times before I got it all right.

I held onto the back of Ray's shirt as he opened the door. Four police officers immediately took him from me and surrounded him as they led him down the two flights of stairs from the apartment. Ray looked back at me one last time as I felt the remaining two officers each grab one of my arms. I didn't even get to say good-bye.

My knees were weak, but one of the officers snapped, "Move it," so I stumbled my way after Ray. Once on the ground floor, I saw Ray in handcuffs and being led to the other end of the alley, where a patrol car sat.

Another patrol car was parked nearby, and I was half-pushed, half-thrown into the back seat. My patrol car went in one direction and Ray's in another, toward the city jail. I never saw him again, the only love I had ever known.

The police didn't tell me where we were going or even

acknowledge my presence. Instead, they talked among themselves, continuing to call me names and make veiled threats about what they would do if they had a daughter like me. Finally, we stopped at the Children's Center, a juvenile detention center.

The tiny room where they took me was anything but child-friendly; rather, it felt like a cell. There was no window or toilet, and a steel door separated me from the gray-haired female warden who sat outside. *What had I done wrong?* I wondered. What law had I broken? If my boyfriend had been white, would they have arrested me? Something told me they wouldn't have.

Fear and panic quickly set in. I began to cry as memories of visiting my brothers in prison came flooding into my mind. I remembered clinging to my mother's hand as the heavy gates slammed closed behind us. I remembered the other men's leering gazes, like caged animals, and fearing my brothers would become like them. As frightening as life in my house could be, in prison, there was no friend's or relative's house to escape to if things got chaotic.

Is that where I was heading after this? What charge would they bring against a fifteen-year-old white girl for loving a black boy?

At some point, the gray-haired lady came in to question me. Her glasses were stationed at the tip of her nose, and her tight bun seemed to pull the flesh tight across her skull. She never made eye contact with me and made certain that I didn't get close to her, as though I was something dirty that she needed to maintain her distance from. Off and on, she glanced at me with a glare in her eyes that made her eyebrows arch.

The warden left again, and I was left to my crazed, worried thoughts for hours. Finally, mercifully, the door swung open once more, and I saw my mother standing before me with a look of disgust and shame upon her face. One of my grown brothers stood at her side, his lips pursed and nostrils flaring.

I ran toward my mother, hoping she would sweep me up in her arms and protect me from this jail where I thought I would be living out my life, but she threw up both hands to stop me in my tracks. There was a thick sense of shame about the room as they murmured to the gray-haired lady about my fate as though I wasn't even present. I knew then that my mother didn't actually believe all the things she had taught me about acceptance of other races—at least not when it came to her daughter.

Eventually, the gray-haired lady unlocked the steel outer door and my brother pointed me through it, again not speaking to me or looking at me. I repeatedly asked, "What are my charges?" but no one would reply.

The drive home seemed to take forever, and no one would listen to me. Every time I tried to speak through tears, I was told to shut up. "Mama, please, I love him," I said.

Finally, she turned around to look at me. "You disgust me."

I didn't try to speak again.

My brother continued not to say anything. He was held in high esteem in our community; everyone was proud of him for making it back from the Vietnam War and for eluding a life in prison like so many of my other siblings. But that pride might easily be taken from him now that he had a race traitor for a sister. I wished that anyone but him had brought Mama to get me.

He dropped us off at our home in the very same housing projects from which I had just been dragged out and taken away. It was like returning to the scene of the crime, so quiet, so dead, as neighbors peered out their windows.

In the coming days, my mother only spoke to me to remind me of how I would go to jail and never see her again. "They're going to put you away forever," she said. "Just you wait. You're gone." She told me that I had to go to court and the judge would send me to one of the many places where my brothers had been locked up, except, according to her, where I was going would be much worse.

But how could anything be worse than where I had seen my brothers locked up? I had been to the Eddyville Penitentiary, the place with the electric chair, where my brother had been locked up for murder. It looked like a wicked castle and was always either too cold or too hot inside. My brother was pale from lack of sun and thin from poor nutrition, and he looked hard and old for his young age.

So when my mother told me that I would spend my life in someplace worse than this, I believed her because I knew prisons were real places and I had been to them all. The worst part of it was that she laughed as she taunted me day after day, "Just you wait until those girls get you." And she still never told me what my charges were.

It was the longest month of my life as I was reminded on a daily basis of my horrors to come. I cried every day waiting for my court date, and when the morning finally came, I was worn out not only from my own tears, but also from my mother's drunkenness and rage, which now felt like my fault. The more she mocked me, the uglier I felt about myself even though I was given no name for the crime I was supposed to feel shame for. The only good thing about my court date would be that I would hopefully get the answers my mother refused to give me as she instead heaped abuse on me.

But when we arrived downtown that day, I was not taken to a courtroom or judge, but rather to a small, dingy conference room in the back of a child welfare office. Several social workers came in and sat across the splintering table from my mother and me.

My nerves got the best of me and I immediately blurted out, "Please don't send me away. I'll be good. I'll go to school and do good. I won't do anything like this again."

They listened to me with slightly bemused expressions, and then, as I started begging them not to send me to jail, they simply burst out laughing.

"You're not going to jail," said a lady in a worn pantsuit. "What makes you think you're going to be sent away?"

I glanced once at my mother and then began pouring my heart out and sharing everything that my mother had said. I was so relieved that I wasn't going to prison, but also so angry at my mother for lying to me that I carried on and on to the social workers about her drinking and being mean to me and about how unhappy I was. I wanted them to straighten her out and get her to stop drinking so she could be the mother I always longed for. But instead, my trust in the social workers backfired on me.

My honesty that day not only cost me my freedom, but also deepened the hatred my mother had for me. A few days after that meeting, at the social workers' decree, I packed a little bag of raggedy clothes and went to live with my father and step-family. The court system thought it was best to remove me from the environment I had described to them, and my mother thought it best to get me as far away from Ray as possible.

At first, being with my father felt like a relief from the torment my mother had been putting me through. After all, I was "the baby," the one my father favored and coddled over my other siblings. I would sit on the arm of his chair and throw my arms around his neck while he watched TV, and I soaked in any scrap of attention he threw my way.

But just as with my mother, my stepmother quickly began to resent me for loving my father and wanting his attention. She glared at me whenever my father and I spoke, and she didn't miss the fact that my father mistreated my stepbrothers and sisters but not me. He ordered them to do everything around the house and was constantly on them for something, but he left me alone. Again I was hated for him loving me over everyone else.

My father and stepmother ran a strict household, and I struggled to adapt to my new life. We had to be in bed by nine o'clock and up at five thirty sharp—a total flip from me being up all night during my mother's drunken brawls. We all had chores we were responsible for without excuse, which was bizarre and suffocating to me after years of living in a home with no rules, structure, or curfew.

Gone were the days of me playing in the streets with neighborhood kids or sitting on the curb listening to music from down the street. I was not allowed to go out of the yard alone except to walk with my stepbrother to school and back. On weekends, I went to church with my stepmother but didn't understand what was being preached to me, whether from the pulpit or the Sunday school teachers. The preacher shouted, flailed his arms, and stomped his feet while he told us that all sinners were bound for hell. Although I was sure I was one of the sinners he was talking about, I had no idea what he expected me to do to escape the hellfire he screamed about.

I was thankful to finally be in a place where I knew there would be food at every mealtime, but I still couldn't help but feel like I was in jail. Before, I had come and gone as I pleased and never known anything other than being left alone to fend for myself. Now, I felt like a wild animal that had been caged and my spirit broken.

And all the while, I was still grieving for the boy I loved. Where had the police taken him? Was he in one of those terrible prisons like my brothers? What would the other prisoners do if they found out he was there for sleeping with a white girl? If they were anything like the Vagrants, he wouldn't make it out alive.

I walked through each day in a daze of depression, and I cried so often that even my stepmother, in spite of all her reasons to hate me, began to take pity on me. One day, she called me into her bedroom. She was standing in front of her antique wardrobe, its doors wide open.

Normally, this wardrobe was strictly off-limits for us kids because the top shelf contained a cubbyhole that was lined with medicines from a long-standing illness my stepmother had. I tried not to show my curiosity, but she was too busy going through her assorted medicines to notice.

"I have something for your nerves, Mary," she said.

She brought out several bottles and shook a few pills into my hands. I had never seen so much medicine, but I recognized Valium and guessed that some of the others were anti-depressants.

"Take one or two of these," she said, "and a couple of those every day. And don't tell your father."

I did as she instructed and soon began taking even more pills than she had told me to take. Two green ones, two brown ones, and several yellow ones every day. I ate them like they were candy, and when I ran out, I went to my stepmother for more.

The pills did help, but perhaps not in the way she intended. I discovered that the drugs allowed me to escape the cage I felt I had been living in. Everything continued as it had before—

chores, school, church, more chores—but I suddenly didn't care so much anymore. Pills, sleep; sleep, pills. Mary didn't have to face anything in the world.

I was now attending the ninth grade, and I went to school looking like I felt—disheveled, wild-eyed, and strained. I tried to do well; in fact, where I had always gotten "Ds" and "Fs" in the past, my grades were coming up in spite of my addled brain.

For six or more months, I walked around the house in a daze, literally stumbling from lack of coordination. Whenever an argument flared about me or my stepsiblings or about my father wanting to disappear for a hunting trip, I would take more pills and sleep to escape. Church became a blur, and the fiery teachings that had at first confused me now terrified me as pictures of cartoon devils and hellfire played like a reel in my mind.

I don't think my father ever knew I was on drugs, and even though she was my dealer, my stepmother had little patience for my slow, drug-induced movements and speech. Finally, one morning when I had taken too many, my stepmother tried to wake me for school, but I couldn't get up fast enough for her. She called my father to bring the belt.

As my father began to beat me, I stumbled out of bed to my feet and then collapsed at the foot of the bed while the belt continued to snap. I looked up at my father as he beat me, but no amount of pain could shake off the weight of the drugs crushing my mind and spirit.

That very day, my father and stepmother decided I was too much trouble and it was time to send me back to my mother. By now, she was living alone in an apartment in the west end of Louisville. Her shame, neglect, and hatred had not changed; if anything, it was worse.

When my father dropped me off at her apartment building, I found my mother sitting at a neighbor's kitchen table with a cigarette in one hand and a beer in the other. Clutching my paper bag full of ratty clothes, I stood in front of her and waited for her to say something, but she had no words of welcome for me. In fact, she didn't speak to me for the next two weeks. I was just there. She would walk off without paying the rent or utilities and leave me alone in the apartment for days, just like when I was little. So I sat by myself, sometimes in the dark or in the cold, with the several bottles of pills that I managed to smuggle home with me from my stepmother.

Eventually, my drug-addled brain remembered my friend Angie, who lived next to the Vagrants biker gang, and I hit the streets in search of her. By then, the Vagrants had moved to the inner city of Louisville, and Dirty Dan was out of prison.

# CHAPTER SEVEN

# The End of an Ice-Cream Season

Finding Angie again felt like the last locks had dropped off the cage of my stepmother's endless routines and chores. I was sixteen now, and the hours of unmonitored freedom promised all new possibilities. My mother didn't seem to care whether I came home at all anymore, so I split my time between Angie's and my brothers' houses, carrying my paper bag of clothes with me everywhere I went. I was back to wondering whether I would have food at each mealtime and where I might be able to shower each day. However, at the time, this familiar chaos felt more comfortable than the strange and strict expectations at my father's house.

Angie still lived next to the Vagrants' old clubhouse, but by the time I came back to her, the biker gang had left the neighborhood and moved downtown. However, their names still loomed large on the street, as if they were local celebrities whom every man wanted to be and every woman wanted to date.

Through the grapevine, I heard that Dirty Dan was out of prison and back in Louisville and was now sporting a bullet wound in his arm. Rumor was that he had been shot by one of his ol' ladies who didn't want to give him what he wanted—and that the bullet had been meant for his chest.

Still, I remembered Dirty's gifts of ice cream and his flirtations, and I could almost hear his baritone voice promising to marry me when he came back. Even just two years ago, I had heard those words through a child's ears. But now that I was a young woman who desired men's attention on a whole new level, it was hard not to blush when I thought about the most handsome man in the Vagrants having his eyes set on me.

I didn't see Dirty in the flesh until one of my rotations of staying with my brother Richard, who was now out of prison after doing time for murder. Richard had really turned his life around; he was married now, and his was one of the better houses I stayed at as I migrated in my search for food and a place to sleep.

Around the corner from Richard's house was the clubhouse of another motorcycle gang. These men reminded me strongly of my days running around Angie's street, back when it was crawling with Vagrants. They partied day and night, and they'd often catcall me when I walked past, skinny and ratty as I was.

But one evening as I walked down the street, a catcall came from a familiar voice. I looked over to see Dirty Dan push himself off the porch, where he had been visiting with some of the bikers, and come striding toward me. He was just as tall and beautiful as I remembered him, with his long hair, striking features, and deep brown eyes.

My heart was beating fast as he leaned over the fence with all his charm and said, "Hey, Mary, I told you I'd be back. Want to go for a ride?"

I was giddy as I accepted and followed him to his chopper.

Even Dirty's bike was the stuff of neighborhood legend. An

elaborate custom paint job decorated the tank with the bike's name ("The Hooker"), and its chrome spokes sparkled in the fading sunlight. Most striking of all was the front-end fork of the bike, which extended more than five feet long, like a shiny battering ram. I had seen it many times parked along Angie's street, but to be so close to it—much less to be touching it— made me feel like the president himself had invited me to ride on Air Force One.

When I climbed on the back of the bike, I didn't know where we would be going or why Dirty Dan was so interested in a scrawny teenage girl whose teeth were still cutting. All I knew was that I was on this famous bike and that this beautiful man wanted me when no one else did.

We screamed through the streets of downtown, and every time we passed a bar, Dirty revved the engine, drawing the attention of the crowds standing outside. Soon we were in Louisville's red light district—an entire four-block radius consisting of more bars, peep shows, and brothels. At the center of it all was the Fillies Theater at the corner of Second and Jefferson, and it was here that we stopped for the first time.

As Dirty backed into the curb, many spectators approached us and attempted to get his attention over the roar of the engine. Recognizing the sound of Dan's bike, many men came out of the closest bar to greet him. It was like being with a celebrity, and my lonely heart soared knowing I was a part of it all.

Dan started chatting with his admirers, leaving me to look at my surroundings. The strangest characters floated all around us. Transvestites and prostitutes wearing very little lurked in dark doorways, and a wino threw up in the gutter across the street. All the buildings had neon signs and twinkling lights that reminded me of a Christmas tree. Signs with triple-Xs were plastered everywhere, and I was so naïve wondering what all the Xs meant.

The marquee of the Fillies Theater read "Girls, Girls, Girls," and it was then I finally understood what Dirty had meant when he told me years before by the ice cream truck that he would put my name in lights. There was a heavy spirit in the air, as oppressive as the stench of smoke, vomit, and alcohol all around us. I was far too young to understand where that night would take me, but I did wonder if this was what the outside was like, what more could possibly lay within these buildings?

Dirty led me through the crowd and inside the Fillies Theater, where it was even darker than the night sky we'd left behind. The carpet was matted under our feet, and the stench of drugs and vomit seemed to double, putting me on my guard.

The old man behind the glass window in the foyer seemed to know Dirty because he waved us through without asking for any kind of payment. We stopped by a small office, where Dirty started talking to another man. This room was no cleaner and barely any lighter, and in the corner was a dark, frightening-looking staircase that led up to the second floor. Thankfully we didn't go up there but instead moved down the hall to a small auditorium, where light from a movie screen illuminated the back of several men's heads as they watched. I quickly realized it was pornography as the sounds of sex crackled through an old sound system.

Dirty and the man from the office stepped away to talk under their breath, and I stared at the floor, trying not to look at the screen or think about what the men in the audience were doing in their seats. After a few minutes, the man from the office hurried upstairs and killed the projector, and suddenly a weak spotlight flickered on and music started to play.

A woman stepped onstage in front of the screen and began to dance. Piece by piece, she removed her clothes, until she was totally nude. I remembered my brother Richard's old girlfriend Regina, who had shown me her costumes just like this woman's and had taught me some of the same dance moves that the lady onstage now employed.

Once her song was finished, another girl took her place onstage, and the first one walked into the crowd of men. One of them stood up and followed her from the theater area, toward that staircase I'd wanted nothing to do with, as another song began to play. Although I didn't really comprehend at the time what was happening, the hair on the back of my neck stood up, and I was beyond relieved when Dirty said it was time to go.

This was how many of my nights passed over the next few weeks—what I came to remember as the honeymoon period. Dirty sported me around like a trophy he had won in a great battle; he showed me off on his motorcycle, in the red light district, and at the Vagrants' clubhouse. Because I was underage, I wasn't allowed inside the clubhouse, so I spent most of my time on the front porch, and Dirty and I slept on a mattress on the floor in the abandoned house next door.

The clubhouse itself was a three-story red brick building with numerous bedrooms to accommodate all the brothers and their ol' ladies. Many of them had no home of their own, and this house provided not only shelter, but also the perfect place for them to host their meetings and throw their parties that lasted for days. The yard was big enough for all the men to chain up their pit bulls and park their bikes. Later, after a rival gang shot at us while we were sitting on the front porch, the brothers built a fence around the front of the building, making it look like a fort. The clientele of the bars and restaurants on the block slowly dwindled away for fear of the Vagrants' activities and crudeness.

I had always wondered what it would be like to be one of the ol' ladies whom Angie and I used to spy on from her bedroom window in Butchertown. Now I was finally one of them. Everything around me was more exciting than anything else I'd ever experienced. Everyone knew who I was, and they even gave me a nickname—Brat, because I was so young and looked even younger with my skinny frame.

Like the rest of them, I started sporting a leather jacket, except that the patch on my back read "Property of the Vagrants: DMFD" (which stood for Dirty MF Dan). I could not have been more proud. Whenever Vagrants from other cities came through town, the brothers would brag, "We raised this one!" and that oddly made me feel more at home than I ever had with my own family.

And the Vagrants were a family—though perhaps a slightly frightening one. These dangerous men had created a world all their own. They all wore jeans, black T-shirts, and leather vests with their Louisville Vagrant patches sewn on them. Everyone wore swastika pins or even had swastikas tattooed on their arms, as they still followed the beliefs of Hitler. Although their views about other races were deplorable, they had a strong sense of loyalty toward one another—a brotherhood and, yes, even a sisterhood too. If ever there was a family in hell, it began with the Vagrants.

I mostly felt like part of the family, but I hadn't been initiated into the sisterhood in one key way. Where the other ol' ladies left the clubhouse every day to work at various strip clubs, peep shows, and massage parlors, I got to stay with Dirty. I sat on his lap and breathed in his sweet scent, all the while feeling like the most adored woman on Earth.

The other brothers sometimes made snide remarks and

asked why I wasn't working. But for the moment—which seemed to be all I was mature enough to comprehend—I focused on the love and burgers and drugs Dirty was providing me. After all, I was special to him, and he had promised to make me a star.

I would have followed that man anywhere. I felt so special when I was with him. He made me feel emotions that I had never felt before. Although small, frantic alarm bells went off in the back of my head every once in a while, it was easy to ignore them when this sweet, loveable, handsome, cool guy looked down at me as if I were the only woman in the world. Beautiful women flocked to him everywhere we went, but he always chose me. For the first time in my life, I thought there must be something special about me, and maybe he saw something in me that I didn't see in myself.

As it always does, the honeymoon period ended, surprising no one but me. I should have known that day would be different, for it was the first time Dirty took me inside the Vagrants' clubhouse. The floors were their original hardwood, but it was sticky and grimy from the men spitting everywhere on it. The walls were covered with iron crosses, swastikas, and patches like the ones they wore on the back of their leather vests. The Vagrant patches were displayed with pride, but the ones they had won from other gangs in fights were nailed upside down.

The first floor was complete with a pool table and a full bar, and although it was still early morning, the party had already started. Everyone was passing around joints of marijuana, and glasses of liquor lined the bar. I got my first taste of Seagram's whiskey dumped inside a mug of coffee (which Dirty liked to call "Irish coffee"), and I accepted the marijuana every time it made its way to me. I sat on a filthy couch studying the patches on the wall while I waited for Dirty to tell me what we were doing that day.

By noon, we were half drunk and very high, and Dirty decided it was time to go. We hopped on his bike and drove downtown to one of the picture booths in the red light district, where men paid to take Polaroid pictures of naked women. I had visited this and many places like it with Dirty, and I had always felt important and grownup to be with him as he chatted and talked business with the managers.

Today, however, everything felt a little different. Several customers crowded the waiting room, and I overheard the manager say that they were short a girl or two. Dirty stepped away to murmur to him, and I tried to keep myself occupied, still enjoying my buzz and trying not to look at any of the men sitting around waiting for their chance to take dirty pictures.

After a few minutes, Dirty returned and said, "I'll be back tonight to pick you up, Mary. Don't worry, the other girls will show you the ropes." He handed me a piece of paper. "Here's the number to the clubhouse. You call if you need anything." Then he bent down to kiss me and left.

I sat stunned and confused for a moment as the manager beckoned me to follow him. I didn't really need the other girls to show me the ropes; I knew what went on here. The drugs coursing through my veins seemed to whisper, "Survive, survive, survive," as I took stock of my pitiful situation: sixteen years old, high, and stranded downtown with nowhere else to go. The other ol' ladies did this and more every day, and I was embarrassed by the thought of Dirty coming back and finding out I had failed when there were plenty of women out there lining up to take my place.

So I stood up and followed the manager, who was sweating for no apparent reason. He led me into the next room, where there was a row of plywood booths, each with walls and a numbered door, but no roof. Music played overhead to deaden the silence and cover the sound of clicking cameras inside the booths. The manager pointed to one of the booths, instructed me to remove all my clothes, and left to tend to all the men waiting their turn to come in here.

Inside the booth was a table, a chair, and some nasty carpet covering the floor. I slowly stripped off all my clothes, piled them on the table, and then sat on the chair and tried to cover myself as much as possible. It seemed like barely a minute had passed before an old man with a fat belly and a sick smile on his face entered, camera in hand. I slowly stood up, hating to put my bare feet on that carpet, but kept my hands crossed over my small breasts.

"You're a pretty little one, aren't you?" he cooed, stepping forward and raising the camera. I took a step backward but soon felt plywood on my bare back. There was nowhere for me to go.

He snapped his first picture and laid it on the table to develop itself. He kept telling me how beautiful I was and asking me to reveal more as he kept snapping, and I did my best to keep as much distance between us as possible.

As each picture popped out of the camera, I suddenly thought about a school project I had finished several weeks ago, when I was the one looking for pictures, not having pictures taken of me. It was for math class; the teacher had told us to look through newspapers for any pictures or mentions of fractions, and we were to cut them out and paste them on a poster board. I'd gotten a "B" on mine, and it was the highest grade I had ever received in my life. Now here I was, with this man taking pictures of me, and who knew where these pictures would end up?

This went on for eight hours. One by one, strangers entered

my little box, never knocking first, so that I was always on edge even when they left me alone. For twenty-five dollars, these men were allowed to come in, all of them with a hungry look about them, and take ten pictures of my sixteen-year-old body. All day long it was nonstop pictures, until I saw spots before my eyes.

Occasionally, I was let out of my box for a bathroom break, but there was nothing to eat or drink, so I used my hands to drink water from the basin in the bathroom. I felt like a doll being tossed in and out of a toy box by big ugly men, and I quickly felt my soul becoming hard and empty, just like the doll—pretty on the outside, nothing on the inside.

Dirty picked me up around eight that evening. He collected the money I'd earned from the manager and took me to get something to eat. Starved, thirsty, and confused, I ate ravenously as Dirty talked to me about continuing to work.

"It will only be for a little while," he said. "You're beautiful and you did so well today—you're a natural. You'll be the best there is by the end of the week, I know it."

The same anxiety I'd felt when he left that morning fluttered in my chest, but at the same time, I was strangely flattered that I seemed to have impressed him. Dirty had done so much for me in such a short time. Out of all the people I lived with—Angie, my brothers, even my own mother—he was the only one who smiled when he saw me and fed me every meal and told me he loved me. How could I say no when he asked only one thing in return?

So I went back, the next day and then the next and then the next. Dirty started giving me sedatives, and I slipped back into the same hazy state I had lived in under my father's roof when my stepmother had given me drugs. The sedatives gave me an "anything-goes" mentality, so wherever Dirty went, I went.

My days got longer when he started to take me to the Fillies Theater after my shifts at the picture booths. Soon I found out exactly what went on up the dark staircase that had disturbed me on my first visit there. One of the older ladies took me back to the dingy office and started schooling me on what took place on the mattress laid out on the floor up there.

"It's easy, baby," she said as she stood in the doorframe, her back against one side and one leg braced against the other at an almost ninety-degree angle. She wore nothing underneath her short, silk skirt, and while she chatted to me, a man in the hallway watched her in open lust, his hand moving vigorously under his pants. She told me what the men would do and exactly what I was to do upstairs, all for the price of thirty dollars.

It was late spring now, and instead of finishing ninth grade, I was learning how to be a prostitute. How had this happened? Everything was moving so fast. I'd known dancers and prostitutes since childhood, but I had never dreamed I'd be one of them. Despite everything that had happened in my life so far, I knew this was truly the end of my innocence. But what I did not know—what I never could have predicted—was that this was only the beginning of a thirty-five-year journey through the sex industry, all thanks to the biker who'd bought me ice cream.

# CHAPTER EIGHT

# The National Meet

B y the time I turned seventeen years old, I had lived on the streets as a homeless and unwanted child, but with the Vagrants, I had found a way to survive. I was a full-fledged ol' lady, living in the clubhouse and working every day in the red light district.

Because I was underage, Dirty moved me around from place to place to avoid any run-ins with the police. My childhood fear of the police and prison was now always on my mind, as I had wild waking nightmares of them bursting in where I was working any given day and hauling me off to one of those prisons where I had visited my brothers. I was afraid of the world, my secrets, and the police, and soon even Dirty—the man who had bought me milkshakes and banana splits and promised to make me a star and marry me—would join the list of things I feared the most.

In addition to the picture booths and the Fillies Theater, I was also working in a bar dancing and hustling drinks. When I wasn't there, I was placed in different triple-X bookstores in the red light district. The first was called Flashers, which housed a small stage with booths built around the edge. Men sat in the booths, and for fifty cents every five minutes, they could watch me dance nude. The ugliness I witnessed in those booths when the money ran out and the lights came back on is still vivid in my mind to this day.

I started to try to find ways to get out of work, either by not going or not cooperating when I was there. But me not working meant Dirty lost out on money, and so when I argued, he began to lash out, hitting me and eventually beating me.

The thought of leaving never occurred to me. By now, I had moved into the clubhouse with Dirty and had nowhere else to go. Besides, I wasn't hungry for once and had all my other needs met. And so I continued to work and handed over all the money I earned to my relatives and to Dirty Dan.

Months went by, and this odd life quickly became routine. Work from noon until four in the morning, sleep all morning, and then do it all over again—with coffee and drugs to keep me going.

My routine changed abruptly one night when Dirty showed up at the whorehouse where I was working at two o'clock in the morning, two hours before my shift ended. The manager docked me a hundred dollars for leaving early, and he told Dirty that because I hadn't made more than a hundred dollars that night, I would be leaving empty-handed. I knew this was a lie so the manager could pocket all the money I had earned, but before I could protest, Dirty slapped me in the face.

Dirty was drunk and high, and he was dangerous to deal with in this condition, just as my mother had been all my life. Since I had spent my childhood dealing with drunks, I thought I knew how to handle grown people in this state—but not even my extensive experience was enough to help me that night.

Dirty was savage as he screamed in my face, "Get your s——; we're out of here. We're leaving town."

"What? Why?" I asked.

He didn't answer, and panic began to set in. "Where are we going, Dirty?" I insisted. "Please don't make me go somewhere I've never been."

"When we get to the clubhouse, you pack a bag. We're leaving tonight."

His tone was so vicious that I was afraid to ask any more. The way he was acting made me think he had done something terrible and we had to get out of town—*now*. In addition to his panic, he was so high that he was sweating bullets. We took off on the chopper in a wheelie and broke the speed limit the entire way to the clubhouse.

Dirty told me to pack the saddlebags and not to take too much, just my dancing gear and some jeans and T-shirts. Unable to help myself, I again asked, "Why?"

His only response was a punch to my head.

We headed down I-65 South and didn't stop until we got to a gas station twenty miles outside of Louisville in the deserted town of Shepherdsville. I could smell the country and the motorcycle fumes, as the bike was hot from Dirty speeding down the highway.

I had never been outside of Louisville before—especially not against my will—and even though the night was still and peaceful around me, my heart wouldn't stop racing. Where were we going? For how long? Were we ever going back? If Dirty had made me work in all those terrible places in Louisville, what would he make me do when I was somewhere I'd never been before, where I had no friends and family to run to?

In tears, I pleaded with him, "Please, Dirty, take me back. I want to go home."

Our helmets were still on from the ride, but when I wouldn't stop crying, Dirty removed his and started beating my head with it. The sound rang like thunder through my helmet, and every now and then, he swung under the face guard and hit my bare skin. He weighed two hundred and forty pounds to my eighty-five, and he was six foot four to my less than five feet.

I hit my knees and held on to the strap of the helmet while I tried to tuck my head into my lap to protect any exposed skin. "Okay, okay, I won't ask again. Please stop," I begged him, sobbing.

Finally, he stopped, and then we were back on the road, still heading south. My head pounded from the beating, and the headache lasted until the next day when we reached Nashville, Tennessee.

When we arrived at the clubhouse of the Nashville chapter of the Vagrants, I was frightened, tired, and hungry as I made a place to sleep on the floor with our sleeping bags. Dirty allowed me to sleep throughout the day, but that evening, he woke me by shoving me in the side with his boot.

"Brat!" he snapped. "Get up! I got a place for you to work. Get up and get your s—— together."

"Where, Dirty?" I asked.

"I don't know. You're going with the other c——s to work in a hotel somewhere." He moved his boot to my back and shoved me again.

"Can you give me a minute and let me wake up, Dirty?" I pleaded as I scrambled out of the sleeping bag and searched for my clothes.

I went into their nasty excuse for a bathroom to wash up in the sink and apply makeup. I chose a thin halter dress from my bag, but before I could even begin to pull it on, Dirty banged on the door and barked, "Hurry up! You better come out of there or I'm coming in."

It made me think of a time at the clubhouse in Louisville when I was taking a bath and Dirty had come into the bathroom to use the toilet. I had my back turned to him while he was urinating, but partway through, he turned and started urinating on my back. I screamed and jumped out of the now-filthy bathwater. Although I was furious and started to yell at him, he just laughed and left me alone again.

Shaking off the memory, I finished pulling myself together and came out of the bathroom. One of the Nashville sisters introduced herself to me and told me I was riding with her, but I still had no clue where we were going.

We ended up at a hotel somewhere in Nashville to work in the lounge. "Work," of course, did not mean waitressing, but finding men to prostitute with. I followed the other girls to the lounge and sat on a barstool. One by one, the other girls disappeared with men to their rooms, leaving me behind to hustle the crowd.

As I sat on the barstool, frightened, angry, and hungry, I let myself fall into despair. I had no money, and I didn't know where I was or if anybody cared. My mother probably didn't even know I'd left the city, and even if I could find a way to get ahold of her, would she come for me? Would she even be able to? I would not have even known what city I was in had I not noticed the patches on the brothers' backs when I was at the clubhouse that morning. I had no identification, and I was only seventeen years old. All I had in this world was an address to give to the cab driver when I was done with work to take me back to Dirty.

A man on the other side of the bar was watching me. I wasn't sure why he took notice of me, as my body language was anything but inviting. My arms and legs were crossed tight, and I was staring down at the bar, pouting.

In spite of all that, he approached me and sat next to me. "You're different from the other girls," he said, trying to get me to look at him.

I focused on the cigarette I was twirling in the ashtray in front of me. "What do you want?" I asked.

"Just to talk."

"So talk."

"Why don't we go somewhere more private?" he said.

*Somewhere more private just to talk? Yeah right.*

"Fine, but you have to pay for the room," I blurted.

"Don't worry, I already have one."

He continued to chat as we made our way to his room. I still couldn't seem to manage to lift my head, so I instead noticed his shoes. They clearly belonged to a man who didn't have much money. Great. Hopefully he at least had my fifty dollars.

We reached his room, and he invited me to sit down at the little table with two chairs facing one another. I began to relax a little. Maybe he did actually just want to talk. He broke out some cocaine and offered me some, and I quickly loosened up and became talkative.

After a little while, he turned the conversation to why he had brought me to the room. "Listen, I'm in the pornography business, and I'm in need of a girl to do a film for me."

"Really?" I said, skeptical. I glanced at his shoes again and wanted to tell him to buzz off, but stopped myself. After all, he was paying me fifty dollars to "talk."

Apparently not noticing my doubts, he continued, "There's a catch to it though."

"What's the catch?" I asked.

"I need a girl to have sex with six black guys."

Every sense in my body immediately became alert. My mind went to my first love, the beautiful black boy I had spent so many peaceful nights with. If the Vagrants ever found out about that, I knew they would kill me for being a race traitor, and I couldn't help but wonder if this man's proposition was some sort of test. Not even Dirty Dan knew about my black boyfriend, so surely this strange man in a strange city couldn't have found out...right?

I did my best to screw up my face in disgust and snapped, "I am *not* that kind of girl. I don't do pornos."

He backed off quickly, and we talked about other things. To this day, I truly believe that if I had said yes to his request, he would have beaten or even killed me. I stayed with him for some time, doing his cocaine and finally falling asleep.

Sometime during the night, the man left, leaving the fifty dollars on the table. When I woke up alone the next day, I took advantage of the relatively clean shower and called a cab. When the cab got there, I handed the driver the address like a child and made my way back to Dirty.

When I reached the clubhouse, Dirty was on the porch with another brother. He looked worried. I said nothing as I climbed up the porch, handed him what was left from my fifty dollars after cab fare, and found my way back to the sleeping bag where I had slept the first night. I still hadn't eaten since we left Louisville.

*

We stayed in Nashville for a couple of weeks before making our way to Charlotte, North Carolina. We lived on bologna sandwiches, slept under expressway overpasses, and bathed in gas stations. The country was beautiful, but the clubhouse in Charlotte was like all the others: dirty, dangerous, and smelling of liquor, marijuana, and sex.

I was beginning to fear that I would never return to

Louisville, but remembering the way Dirty had beaten me with his helmet, I kept my anxieties and questions to myself. Dirty was the only familiar face in a world of strangeness, and I clung to him no matter what he did to me.

At the Charlotte clubhouse, there was another Vagrant brother in from out of town, from Atlanta, Georgia. His name was Trash, and he was kind to me and always told me what a great job I did when I shaved his head for him. Starved for praise and attention as I was, I began fetching his food and drinks (prepared by the other ol' ladies), and in exchange, he told me funny stories and complimented me as if I had cooked the food myself.

I craved his kindness and approval, and he never addressed me by that ugly name, "c———." All the women were beckoned by this name. No matter what chapter house we visited, all the men used it. The drunker the men got, the more you heard that word, and you answered to it or else.

When it was time to head out on the road again, Trash joined us, as well as a probate who tagged along with Dirty Dan. The probate was very young and had a strong Carolina accent. Now that there were more of us, we needed more food and supplies, so we started stopping at truck stops so I could make money for us through prostitution.

Dirty and the other men would park their bikes out of sight while I was instructed to do as I was told or take a beating for not obeying. Dirty watched me from a distance as I climbed in and out of trucks to service their drivers, all the time feeling shallow and hopeless and wanting desperately to go home. However, if I wanted to eat and stay alive, I had to sell my body while three grown men stood aside and waited on me to make enough money to satisfy Dirty.

Somewhere along our journey, in the office of one of the

brothels I was put in for the night, I found an index card and made a postcard for my mother. I had picked some four-leaf clovers earlier that day because I knew she loved them, and I taped them next to a poem I wrote for her. I scribbled my brother Richard's address on it and prayed she would receive it somehow.

Would she know or care that I loved her and missed her? Would she wonder if I was dead or alive? I fantasized about coming home to her and all the things we would do together—even though I knew she had abandoned me to this life, and even though I was not certain I would ever make it home alive.

After many days of traveling and prostituting, we were rumbling down another new road, deep into the country of North Carolina. It was a nice day out, and we were riding without helmets, so that my hair streamed and whipped around me with each turn. After a while, I mustered up the courage to ask, "Where are we now, Dirty?"

"Love Valley, Brat," he answered over the roar of the bike.

We finally came upon a log cabin, where several motorcycles were already parked. My hair was wild and my butt sore from riding for so long, and we smelled like gas and sweat from being on the road for days. I was told to use the bathroom in the woods, and if I wanted to bathe, do it in the creek. No phone, no town nearby, nothing but nature and more Vagrants.

The brothers' patches were from several different cities, but I couldn't read well enough to make out what they all said. For maybe a month or so, we stayed in Love Valley, sleeping under the stars and eating lunch meat for every meal. I was just relieved that I didn't have to work while we were there. For once, there were no dirty brothels, no scary clubhouses, no nasty truckers to entertain.

After Love Valley, we went on to our final destination and the whole purpose of our journey: a National Meet that the Vagrants were hosting in Durham, North Carolina. The meeting was "mandatory"—one of the first words I learned from the bikers that contained more than four letters, and a word that Dirty taught me because it came up often with the Vagrants.

The meet took place on an empty piece of farmland outside the city. I had never seen so many Harley Davidsons at one time in one place. Just as it always did in Louisville, Dirty's tricked-out bike drew the most attention from the other brothers. However, to Dirty's displeasure, they called it "pretty" because of all its accessories and paint jobs.

Unlike Dirty's bike, we looked far from pretty after our days on the road. My bag of belongings consisted of clothes and shoes I had collected from other ol' ladies we had met along the way. Dirty had gotten a tent from someone, and when we set it up among all the others, we quickly discovered it had holes in it. It rained that first night, and we slept in a puddle, our bodies shivering and teeth chattering.

The next day, I hung out the sleeping bags to dry in the heat as the field began filling up with more bikers and even more supplies. A refrigerated truck filled with meat arrived. A U-Haul came packed with food and cooking supplies, and yet another truck contained several kegs of beer with taps sticking out the sides of the truck.

A grill the size of a car stood in the middle of the field, and it had been roped off to keep people from the food and hot coals. Dirty told me to go join a couple of other girls who were already grilling meat. As the heat from the grill hit me like a wall, I had a brief flashback of the time the hot coals had destroyed the bottoms of my feet. In addition to the fire and smoke from the grill, the Carolina sun beat down on us all afternoon, making for nearly unbearable work.

For the duration of the day, I was corralled in my little roped-off inferno until finally I heard Dirty's voice yell out over the crowd. "Brat, get out of there and come get something to drink and hang with me and the fellas."

Delighted, I jumped over the rope, grabbed myself a soda, and walked with Dirty over to where some brothers were playing cards on a huge tree stump. The tree itself, its leaves still green and full, was lying on the ground nearby. The bikers had cut it down just to make a table for themselves, and I remember being sad for the tree.

The men playing cards had patches on their backs from all over the United States and even Canada. I had met plenty of out-of-towners when they came through Louisville, but I had no idea there were so many and from all around the country.

While standing among the men in the card game, I noticed a tattoo on one of their arms of a nail and hammer that crossed each other. "What do the nail and hammer mean?" I asked him, interrupting his card playing like a precocious child.

He paused for a moment as he discarded a card to the center of the tree trunk and then said, "That's from when I nailed a c—— to a tree."

"You what?" I asked, shocked.

"You heard me right! That's when I nailed a c—— to a tree." Then he added, "My buddy helped me."

He called another man over and told him to show me the same tattoo of a nail and hammer on his arm. I couldn't believe what I was hearing as I imagined the pain the girl must have endured being nailed to a tree. *Just like Jesus*, I thought to myself.

"Did you go to jail?" I asked.

"Well, yeah," he said. He continued to play his cards and

answer my questions as if he were making out a grocery list.

"How much time did you do?"

"Six months."

"Six months!" I repeated, shocked.

"Yeah, that's all the time you get for nailing a c——— to a tree." He cocked his head and smiled out of the corner of his mouth as if he enjoyed what he had just said.

I stood there for a while, my month hanging open, until Dirty turned to me and barked, "Get busy picking up trash or something. Just stay out of the fellas' way and stop asking so many questions before you get the brakes beat off you."

Somewhat relieved, I wandered away. Nursing my soda, I sat under a tree and watched as the evening turned into night. As the darkness fell, the brothers made the biggest fire I had ever seen. They threw object after object on it until it roared nearly twenty feet high. I watched until I caught sight of Dirty and stuck with him next to the fire while they continued to party late into the night.

The next day, it was work, work, work for the women and party for the men. If a total stranger asked you for a beer, you fetched it, or if he told you to make him food, you did it. We were mere slaves to facilitate their hedonism.

This went on for several days. I worked so hard and sweat so much in the summer heat that the days blended together, and I had no idea when it would all end. But then one afternoon, everyone started to pack up, leaving a ruined field behind, and hundreds of bikes roared to life as we headed out in one great pack. There were so many of us that the local police escorted us to the border of their district to keep traffic under control.

A little outside of Durham, the pack stopped, and several people started shouting and getting off their bikes. Dirty ordered me off our bike and pointed me to a large truck that sort of looked like a square bread truck. "Get in the truck. We're in Prince territory."

Petrified, I followed the other women into the truck. The Princes of Darkness were another biker gang with a long history of rivalry with the Vagrants. Actually, *rivalry* is a tame word for what these bikers did to each other if they found the other gang in their territory. Beatings and broken bones were the best we could hope for, and bullets were the worst.

The Vagrants had turned their quasi-bread truck into something of a tank. Each side panel had four square holes cut into it, and there were two more holes in the back. Once the women were all in the truck, we were instructed to sit down in a circle in the middle of the floor. Then several men bearing machine guns took up positions along the outer panels and stuck the tips of their guns out of the holes. The driver had a pistol in one hand and the wheel in the other, and the passenger had a sawed-off shotgun. It was like something out of a movie, except that our lives were actually on the line.

That truck ride ended up feeling like the longest part of this horrible, awful journey. The women were crammed in so tightly that my muscles cramped from not being able to move, and the air was so stale and hot that I felt like I wasn't getting any oxygen no matter how deeply I breathed. We could have gotten killed at any time, and I was convinced more than ever that I would never see my mother again.

I promised myself then that if I lived long enough to get back home to Louisville, I would never, ever leave again.

# CHAPTER NINE

# Given Away Again

We made it through the Princes' territory without incident, and once the women had unloaded from the bread truck, we started to go our separate ways. One by one, the bikes disappeared down different highways taking them back to where they had come from.

I again didn't know where we were going and was not allowed to ask, so I was left to hope and pray that each route we took was bringing me closer to home. It was 1977, and it had been at least half a year since I had seen anyone or anything I knew and loved. To this day, I don't know what it was that night that forced Dirty to leave Louisville so suddenly, but it had to have been something ugly for him to take us on this wild journey that seemed to have no destination or purpose.

We rode nonstop, returning to the same rest areas and truck stops we had visited months prior. We were back to living on lunch meat, and I didn't mind this too much until I began to vomit it back up every day. If the bike vibrated the wrong way or I smelled something off, I would lose the contents of my stomach. I thought I had the flu, but Dirty knew better. We were far away from Louisville, and without my mother or anyone else to guide me, I had no idea that I was pregnant—just that I was feeling terrible.

What I also didn't know was that Dirty was starting to make plans to ditch me now that I was "damaged goods." I overheard him telling another brother, "We'd keep it if we knew it was mine, but there's no telling." I didn't know what to make of that comment at the time, but I know now that he didn't want to be with a woman who might be carrying another man's baby. Never mind that it was under his orders that I had done what led to this pregnancy. Never mind that those acts were what had fed us these last long months on the road. All Dirty cared about was that I wouldn't make him as much money anymore now that this child was growing inside of me.

In spite of being pregnant, I was ten pounds lighter than I had been when we left, coming in at a mere seventy-five pounds. My skin had tanned from living on the back of the bike, and my features were haggard from dealing with morning sickness with no one but bikers and the open road for comfort.

We continued traveling day and night, and although I'd never really learned to read well, I recognized the word *Tennessee* on a road sign and then *Bowling Green, Kentucky.* We were getting closer.

We stopped at an amusement park a couple of hours outside of Louisville, where yet another huge party was taking place. Like the National Meet, it was a biker party that was so big and so wild that it made national headlines that year.

We rode into the park, and again bikes were everywhere. We finally found an open spot under a tree. Dirty unloaded the bike and then took off into the park, leaving me behind alone, filthy, hungry, and tired. As I lay under the tree in my sleeping bag, I listened to the sounds of the party and hoped and prayed that we were on the road to home. Little did I know that just a few hundred yards away, Dirty was finishing up his plans to get rid of me.

The next morning, Dirty showed up to our tree with another girl. She was from New York, with a heavy accent to match. She drove a new car and appeared healthy, happy, and well dressed—unlike me or any of my Vagrant sisters.

Confused but with a growing sense of dread, I looked between the two of them and waited for someone to explain.

No pity in his eyes, Dirty pointed at the woman and said, "Take off your patch and give it to her."

"What?" was all I could say. My patch ("Property of Vagrants: DMFD") was my lifeline in the Vagrants' world. It was the mark of my enslavement to Dirty, yes, but it was also what kept other men from raping and abusing me, because they knew if they messed with me, they were messing with Dirty Dan. The patch was also the thing I had thought was so cool when I was a child—the thing that made me feel like I belonged somewhere for the first time in my life.

"You're not my ol' lady anymore, Brat," Dirty said. "You're Rooster's now. He's going to take you back to Louisville, and you'll do whatever he says."

And there, under that tree, when I should have been relieved that I was finally going back home, I began to cry. The man who had bought me ice creams and made me feel so special was now rejecting me for this tall, beautiful woman who was everything I could never be. I pulled off my beloved patch and handed it to her. Through my tears, I said, "Take care of it and don't lose it. It may be the one thing that keeps you safe."

The worst and most humiliating thing that could happen to a club member was to be stripped of his patch. That was why the Vagrants hung other biker gangs' patches upside down on their clubhouse walls—to show that they had conquered and degraded them. And now it was happening to me.

Dirty ordered me to get on the back of Rooster's bike, and I did as I was instructed. Rooster took me to a motel in town to shower and rest, leaving Dirty and his new ol' lady back at the park partying.

I couldn't stop crying. Although I wanted more than anything to go home, I had no idea what I was going home to now. At least with Dirty, I had a home at the Vagrants' clubhouse, but everything was different now. Where would I go once I got back to Louisville? Who would take me in now that I was a harlot unwanted even by her own pimp?

No matter how dysfunctional my family was, I longed to be in their presence again, especially my mother. But did she feel the same way about me? Had she thought about me this whole time I had been gone? She had abandoned me time and again throughout my childhood, and what made me think things would be different this time, especially now that I had gone to so many terrible places and done so many terrible things? A nasty, despicable biker thought I was damaged goods. Why would anyone else think any different?

*

That night in the hotel, Rooster showed me sympathy where Dirty had shown none. Like most Vagrants, Rooster was known to beat his women for very little. But for some reason, I was spared. Although we slept in the same bed, I couldn't bring myself to let him touch me. I pulled away when he would reach for me, for I had had enough of being turned out. And mercifully, he never forced his way on me.

The next morning as we were getting ready, Jackson Browne's "Running on Empty" was playing on the radio, and I knew that song was meant for me.

Soon we were back on the road, and when we passed under the sign that read "Louisville," I screamed, "Yes!" and raised my fist as if I had won some sort of race.

My heart seemed to swell bigger and bigger with each mile of Louisville road under me. After everything I had survived the past six months, I felt I could get through anything once I was back home.

My confidence was at its peak when we arrived at the Louisville clubhouse. Rooster backed the bike up against the curb, and before he could park completely, I hopped off, took off his helmet, and laid it on the ground. I grabbed my little garbage bag containing all I had in the world and began to walk away.

"Hey!" Rooster shouted. "Where are you going? You're my ol' lady now. Dirty Dan gave you to me."

I turned around and shouted back, "Go to hell, Vagrant! I don't belong to anyone but me!"

Then I took off running.

I cannot describe the feeling of having Louisville under my feet. Although I had no home, at last I was on familiar ground. This was where I had gone to school, this was where I had friends, and this was where, hopefully, at least one family member would love me enough to take me in.

When it was safe enough to stop running, I slowed down and let happiness wash over me as I literally skipped through the streets of downtown. I slung my plastic bag over my shoulder and savored the feel of the Louisville streets on the soles of my dirty, worn-out Chuck Taylor tennis shoes.

I took the long walk from Second and Kentucky Street to Twenty-Sixth and Bank in the west end of Louisville. I walked more than thirty blocks to find my brother Richard, who knew what pain was all about from the time he spent in prison for murder. He took me in with welcoming arms.

I was seventeen and had been with Dirty for more than a year. I didn't tell Richard or anyone else about my journey or what I had done to survive. I was home, and I was not going to do anything to risk being given away again.

*

Thanks to the Vagrants, I now knew how to provide for myself, and I was going to hit the streets of the red light district to do it. Although underage, I took to the strip clubs and the peep shows, and I felt powerful and important knowing that I was doing this for me now, not some dirty old biker. I was going to show everyone that I could take care of myself, and I wanted to prove to everyone who had turned their backs on me that I could survive, doing what I had been conditioned to do.

My mother, Tucker, and some of my other grown siblings were all living in a rented house in the east end of Louisville. It turned out that while I had been on the road, my mother had lived out of a bag just like me. She went from house to house and refused to have a home of her own, because once she did, her children would come to her looking for money and a free place to crash. Everyone's issues were too much for her to bear, and so she instead chose to remain homeless for a time.

However, by the time I got back from the road, she and Tucker had settled down again and predictably had several people living with them. Once Richard told me where she lived, I went to visit right away. After months of longing to see her, I thought my mother would have a million questions and be ecstatic to welcome me home, but the best I could get was a conversation about renting a room in her house.

I did, however, discover that Mama had received the

postcard I had made for her while on the road. Richard had made sure to give it to her, and she told me she enjoyed it. Although it was the smallest sign of affection from her, it made me happy to know she liked something I had made for her.

Reuniting with my mother also helped me diagnose what I had thought was the flu as I traveled home. My mother immediately recognized that I was pregnant and told me she would help me take care of it. She took me to the abortion clinic, and I submitted to the doctors terminating the little life within me.

Abortion was such a common thing to the women in the red light district that I didn't really think much of it at the time. Besides, my childhood had been so terrible that I wanted nothing to do with bringing a child into the hellhole I had been scraping out of the last seventeen years. The other women in the clubs claimed they didn't care or think much about their own abortions, but somewhere deep in my heart, I could never forget or ignore this little soul who had lived inside me.

Although I was making hundreds of dollars a night, I was too young to rent a place of my own, so I moved in with my mother and the rest of the family. Wanting to carry my own weight in the household, I continued working every day, just as I had with the Vagrants. And just as with the Vagrants, the money I earned seemed to disappear more often than not. Tucker and I were the only two bringing in money and seeing to the financial needs of everyone else who lived there.

While we worked, the rest of the family for the most part remained like before—stoned, drunk, or high. The money I earned from the clubs was enough to buy food for my entire family and give Mama money for rent, and everyone knew it. I was so naïve that everyone knew how to take advantage of me. Although I worked from noon until four in the morning every day, they would wake me up from my few precious hours of sleep to ask to borrow money, or sometimes they wouldn't even bother with that and would just steal it out of my purse. They never repaid me, but I didn't get too upset because I knew I would always make more the next day.

In the 1970s, anyone making the kind of money I was making could have really gone places. But I didn't know what to do with the money I was bringing home every night, so whatever was left over after my family hounded me, I spent on frivolous things. I went clothes shopping for the first time, but I had no sense of fashion and didn't know how to dress or pick out cute clothes like my girlfriends. Color coordinating didn't make sense to me, and I wasn't sure what size I was, so I just invested my money back into the costumes that I wore onstage at the strip clubs. But the most important thing to me was that I ate well, and after years of missing meals as a child, I made sure to treat myself now that I could control when and what I ate.

Shortly after I got back to Louisville, I made my way back to Baby Dolls, the first strip club I had worked for at the age of sixteen. The old manager was the one who had taught me how to play the game when I first started working there, and now, a year and a half later, I was living by his advice.

"You can hustle the men and make just as much money without having sex with them," he had said.

And indeed, I could hustle drinks and make as much money as any other stripper, but when it came to selling my body, I was too afraid of the police to do anything that extreme. I would talk to men and flirt with them, suggesting promises of sexual favors as they bought me drink after drink, but never following through. It was better than working at the disgusting peep shows downtown, and I would have taken the strip clubs any day over the appalling things I witnessed in those booths.

As good as I was at my job, I was still nothing compared to the star strippers who traveled around the region because there was such high demand for their talents. Their costumes were beautiful and their dance routines glamorous, and I wanted so much to be like them. I wanted to make lots of money and rent my own place and keep the promise I had made to myself as a child—that I would take care of myself and always have a home with a refrigerator full of food. I wasn't going to be a drunk or do drugs; I just wanted to have the pretty things that normal people had, and I didn't want the world to know how dumb I was. So I pretended to be special and important in the club. There, I felt loved by the other dancers, who were older than me and who treated me like the baby of the family.

I also found a little bit of love from a boy I met while working in the clubs. He was nineteen years old and every girl's blue-eyed dream. We dated for a short time, and I deluded myself thinking I could have a normal teenage life with him outside the red light district. However, his friend soon convinced him that I was nothing more than the harlot I had come to be, and that same friend came into the bar without him to inform me that my blue-eyed boyfriend had wanted me only for sex and nothing more.

Although the relationship hadn't lasted long, it confirmed all of my worst fears: that prostitution and hustling drinks were all that I was good for and that Dirty Dan was my only chance at ever being loved. This whole lifestyle was starting to feel normal to me. No education, no talents, no shot at life. The skill of hustling and conning, day after day and year after year, was something I was coming to master and hate at the same time. I didn't know what "normal" adult life was like outside of this world I had been thrust into, but I wanted it, badly. All I knew was that normal wasn't down here in the dirt with tricks and perverts.

But no matter how much you hate it, the sex industry always seems to find a way to pull you back in. I found this out the hard way while working one night at Baby Dolls. It was my turn to go onstage, and the manager had allowed me to wear one of the dresses owned by the club. It was made of nothing but beads—no other material at all except for the zipper and a thin strip of cloth that ran the length of the dress. The beads draped around my body, and prisms danced off the dress whenever I moved.

I heard the emcee announce my stage name. "Lookie, lookie, gentlemen, here comes Cookie!"

The music to Aretha Franklin's "Respect" played, and the curtains rolled back to reveal me standing there in all my glamour. I stepped out onstage, dragging a white boa behind me. As I danced, I flipped the boa around me, and occasionally I stopped and pulled out a feather to blow to the customers. As the feather floated down from the stage, they would fight for it, and I knew I was the most powerful woman in the room. I strutted around as though I was the star Dirty had always promised me I would be, and I felt special as all eyes in the house were fixed on me.

As I glided down the runway, I looked into the audience to try to judge who my biggest tippers might be. But what I found nearly stopped me in my bead-filled tracks. There, among all the hungry-looking men in the crowd, was Dirty Dan.

# CHAPTER TEN

# The Wedding

My heart was pounding, and I pretended not to notice him. But Dirty knew that I had seen him. I tried to focus on finishing my dance, all the while knowing that there would be no escaping him once it was over. It was, after all, my job to entertain men like him.

And sure enough, once the set was over, Dirty walked up to the stage. I wasn't sure what he could have to say to me after abandoning me like he had, but anxiety and anticipation seized me all the same as I waited for him to speak.

But all he said was, "Call me at the clubhouse sometime," and then he walked away.

I should have told him I would never call him and he was beyond arrogant to think I would. But instead, I just stared after him, speechless. I should have hated him with everything in me, but instead, my heart was screaming, *I need you to love me!* He had given me away just as my mother had, and everything I wanted from her, I also wanted from him—no matter the cost.

So the next day, I called him. I no longer carried the child I had become pregnant with while he was pimping me out, but in its place was a grudge I could not shake. I longed to hear him throw himself at my feet and beg for mercy for doing what he had done to me, but all I got from him was more of the same flirting and flattering that had started back when we were standing beside the ice cream truck. I wasn't sure why I thought he would be remorseful—after all, no one else in my life had ever apologized to me, so why would it start now with this Vagrant? But his compliments did just enough to soothe my bruised and aching heart, and so began Dirty's journey back into my life.

Before long, Dirty tracked down not only the club I worked in, but also the house where I now lived with my family. My family thought he was so cool; whenever he arrived on his chopper, they would stop whatever they were doing, run outside, and gather around him and his bike. It was like we were in Butchertown again, where the Vagrants were larger than life and Dirty Dan was the coolest of them all.

This pattern continued for months, and with each passing day, I let Dirty back in a little bit more. Eventually, my mother gave up having a house again, and I returned to moving from relative to relative, living anywhere I could hang my heels— including the Vagrants' clubhouse. Although it would take months, I finally went back to living with—and working for— Dirty full time.

Even years later, I never completely understood why Dirty wanted me back so much that he would pursue me the way he did. After all, he had given me away to another Vagrant, and when he first found me in the club, he was still with the sophisticated girl he had met in Bowling Green. I believe he was impressed that I didn't stay with the man he had sent me home with that horrible day. Most ol' ladies, once sold or given away, stayed with whomever they were purchased by or given to. No one—least of all ol' ladies—walked away from the

Vagrants like that.

Life with Dirty after the National Meet was much like it had been before. I kept working at the same places, but now, instead of handing over money to my family, I was handing it all to Dirty. And if I didn't make enough, I could expect a beating when I got home. It was a terrible cycle; while I was at work, my stomach churned at the thought of doing some of the things all the other girls were willing to do, but then by the end of my shift, my stomach was churning at the thought of going home empty-handed. Still, through all of that, I was hoping that Dirty would love me when no normal man would and that he would make up for the terrible wrong of abandoning me. His pursuit to get me back made me feel good sometimes, but ultimately, I still harbored anger in my heart.

I was also back to witnessing the Vagrants' nasty and hedonistic behaviors day in and day out. While Dirty was still seeing the girl from Bowling Green, the brothers put a dead cat in her brand new car, where it baked for three days in ninety-degree heat. After they peeled it out, Dirty tried to spray the interior with all kinds of cleaners and even some perfume, but nothing helped. When he picked me up from work, it was bad enough that he had come in another woman's car, but the smell was so unbearable that I had to hang my head out the window to breathe fresh air on the whole drive home.

This kind of cruelty to animals happened all the time among the Vagrants. Many of them had pit bulls that lived and fought in the clubhouse's backyard, even deep into the winter months. The winter of 1977 was a particularly cold one that brought several feet of snow, but still the dogs remained outside. One of the dogs belonged to Gunner, a brother whom the other ol' ladies and I liked a lot because he was kind-hearted and treated women well. This conduct, of course, earned him nothing but ridicule from the other brothers.

So when Gunner's dog froze to death one night, Dirty and another brother decided to play a joke on him. They sawed off the dog's head, fixed her face to make it look like she was growling, and then placed the head on the mantel of the clubhouse's bar. Then they called Gunner and told him to come over to party.

Since he lived close by, Gunner showed up shortly afterward, and everyone watched him, waiting for him to discover his beloved dog's head. It took him a while to notice, as the room was full of Christmas decorations, including a tree decorated with used tampons and a douche bottle on top where the angel was supposed to be.

Finally, Gunner's eyes fell on the mantel, and the other brothers began to howl with laughter. Gunner tried to restrain his emotions, as it was unwise to show weakness in front of everyone like this, but he could not contain his anger. He started screaming and accusing the brothers of killing his dog, but Dirty assured him that the dog had been dead before they decapitated her, as if that made it all right.

Although I kept my thoughts to myself, I was sick to my stomach watching this kind brother and didn't think any part of it was funny. The cruder the brothers were, the more class they thought they had. No one was ever safe, because you never knew what was going to happen when they were looking for ways to entertain themselves.

Unfortunately, the brothers weren't the only ones to display such cruelty that winter. After the cat incident, the Bowling Green woman left for good, but soon another mistress would take her place in Dirty's life. And she would bring out an evil in me I have never encountered before or since.

It started one night when I came home from the bar early. I

knew Dirty would be angry that I hadn't made much money, but I was sick of working and just wanted to relax at the clubhouse. Once I arrived, though, I found Dirty with his new mistress, who was much older and prettier than I was. He had been cozying up to her in hopes that she would be another ol' lady who would give him money and buy things for him.

When I realized what was going on, I cursed her out in front of everyone and threatened her until she left the clubhouse. Everyone just watched, speechless. This was something the other ol' ladies would never do, let alone escape without a beating. Many of the Vagrants' women were beaten for showing any sign of power, but I was forever speaking my mind. I was already in trouble for coming home early with very little money, so I figured I had little to lose, and when I found her there, I let my pride get the best of me.

But that night, neither Dirty nor the other brothers did anything, so I left the clubhouse, thinking I had gotten away with making her leave. Dirty and I were staying with a brother who lived down the street, so I went there and lay down on the couch to sleep. It was about three in the morning, and I was exhausted from working since noon.

Meanwhile, Dirty and his brothers continued to drink at the clubhouse and then at the bar on the corner when it opened at six in the morning. One of the brothers must have made a comment to Dirty about him letting me mouth off like I had, and so he spent those hours stewing about me not making money and running off his potential sugar mama.

Finally, at about seven in the morning, Dirty returned to our house in a drunken rage, accompanied by several brothers. I was fast asleep on the couch when he grabbed me by the hair and punched me in the face. I woke with a shock as he punched me again, and I began pleading for him to stop. The brothers with him stood by as usual and watched as if domestic abuse were a sport.

Dirty dragged me off the couch and onto the floor and began stomping on me with his boots. He outweighed me by nearly two hundred pounds, so the only advantage I had over him was the fact that I could outrun him, but not with a room full of men guarding the doors. Both my eyes were blackened and swollen, and my ribs felt broken as I held up both hands and struggled to my knees to plead for my life.

Dirty eventually let up and returned to the clubhouse with his brothers. And I was left with the task of figuring out how to cover my bruised face with makeup so I could return to work as soon as possible.

Later that week, I was driving home from the bar in a tiny car Dirty bought for me so I could get myself back and forth from work. The snow was deep, forcing me to drive slowly. The bruises from my beating had disappeared enough that makeup could now cover them somewhat, so I had been sent back to work as soon as I could camouflage what had happened to my face.

It was in the early hours of the morning when I came upon a car that was wrecked into a fence. The engine was still running and blowing steam from the radiator. The front end was totaled, and I knew whoever was inside had to be hurt. There was no other traffic, and the snow seemed to have silenced everything but the sound of the radiator spewing.

Concerned, I pulled over. I wasn't too far from the clubhouse, and as I trod through the snow to get to the wrecked vehicle, I realized with dread that the car looked familiar. I had seen Dirty drive a car just like this one.

I reached the driver's side front door and took a deep breath to prepare myself for what I might find. But it wasn't

Dirty I found when I opened the door.

Instead, it was Dirty's mistress—the girl I had cursed and threatened earlier that week. I hadn't run her off after all; she must have been coming from or going to the clubhouse to visit Dirty while I was off working to support us both. I had paid for my sins with a beating in my sleep, but here she and Dirty were back to running around on me no matter what I said or did.

The woman's face was busted up, and she was clearly drunk. She was mumbling something through her bloody mouth. I couldn't understand her, but she must have been asking for help.

This woman who had caused me so much pain—both physical and emotional—was now at my mercy. I should have called for help, but instead, I sneered, "Go to hell, b———," and slammed the car door, leaving her stranded and in need of medical attention.

It was the only time in my life that I remember being so evil. Later, I found out she was okay and even saw Dirty driving that same car with its wrecked front end. But even as he continued hurting and betraying me, I never told him of my vengeance.

*

I continued to stay with Dirty through the beatings and the unfaithfulness, the work and the grime. For months, I was an ol' lady just like all the others until the summer of 1978, when Dirty arranged for me to be his wife.

One afternoon, without really consulting me, he dragged me down to the courthouse to get a marriage license and then to the clinic to get our blood tests done. I had no interest in marrying him, but it seemed I had no choice in the matter.

After all, Dirty was the one who controlled where I went, and since I was still only seventeen years old, my mother legally had to sign off on the marriage—which she did enthusiastically. No one asked what I wanted in the whole process, and so, like most everything else in my childhood, I submitted to those around me, no matter how unhappy it made me.

Most girls love planning their own weddings. They love picking out the venue, meeting with the minister, planning the reception, and finding the perfect wedding dress. But that was not how my wedding to Dirty worked. There would be no pretty dress or church for me, but rather a seedy bar on the corner near the clubhouse that the Vagrants had slowly taken over and made their own. Dirty was the one who planned it, announced it, and saw to it that everyone showed up for his big day. In the days and weeks leading up the wedding, he invited literally everyone we encountered as we traveled around the city while I stood by quietly.

And they did show up—hundreds of people, including the Vagrants and their ol' ladies, the judge who married us, the lawyers who drew up our marriage contract, and many other strangers besides them. Although my mother had signed me away to this man, neither she nor any other member of my family came to see me married.

Most brides spend the morning of their wedding getting ready with their girlfriends, but as for me, I just put on blue jeans, boots, and a black T-shirt with my property patch slapped on the back. Dirty wore his typical biker leather. The bar where we got married used to be a classy establishment because of its grand marble-floored dance hall in the back, but by the time of our wedding, it was run down and infested with clientele like the Vagrants.

When I showed up that day and entered the bar area, I was

greeted with a large, blown-up picture of myself taken by one of the peep show's frequent customers. The picture had always been a favorite of Dirty's, and he had chosen our wedding day to have it made life size and hung over the mirror behind the bar among all the liquor bottles. I was naked in the picture, but you couldn't really see anything inappropriate; rather, it was more of a silhouette shot of me sitting with my knees up by my breasts and looking off into the distance, with my lower lip puckered out as if I was unhappy to be there.

I was quickly ushered back to the dance hall, where the ceremony was to take place. I remember smiling nervously at all these strangers surrounding me; I didn't really want to be there, but since I was the bride, everyone was being so nice to me and paying me more attention than I'd ever received.

Vagrants flanked Dirty and me as we recited our vows. I repeated the words that the minister told me to say without any real thought or feeling. It was just another day of Dirty telling me what to do and me obeying.

As soon as we said "I do," two of the brothers stepped around in front of us and hit us both in the forehead with eggs they had been clutching behind their backs. Yolk slapped us both in the face and dripped down onto our clothes. Dirty was furious, but I just laughed at him. If this was the worst practical joke I could expect on my wedding day, then I considered myself a lucky woman.

But it turned out that wasn't the only Vagrant joke I would encounter that day. Less than half an hour after I vowed to be his wife, Dirty presented me with a marriage contract drawn up by our lawyers. It stated that I was Dirty's slave and he was my master and that I was to—just to name a few things—cook and carry his food to him every meal, bring home all the money for our marriage, and wash and wax his beloved chopper whenever he wanted.

Dirty laughed as I struggled to read each line and became increasingly more distressed. It was supposed to be a joke, but I was so intimidated by lawyers and anything to do with the legal system that my emotions were running high—especially when I saw a real notary stamp on the contract. Being the immature and rebellious child that I had come to be, I threw the contract in Dirty's face and shouted, "I'm not doing anything this says!"

Angry that I had ruined his joke in front of everyone, Dirty balled his fist and punched me in the face. My eye immediately started to swell and blacken, and the lawyers—these men who should have been the first people to defend and protect abused women like me—just watched without comment.

The reception continued at the bar well into the night. I drank whiskey until one of the other ol' ladies had to carry me the two blocks and three flights of stairs back to where Dirty and I were staying. When I woke up later that night, Dirty was lying next to me. He roused too, and as we looked at one another, I saw that he had a black eye to match mine. After Dirty had hit me for throwing the contract at him, the Vagrant club president had taken him aside and punched *him*—not because Dirty had abused me less than thirty minutes after marrying me, but because he had done it in front of the authorities.

So there we were, two newlyweds gazing at each other through blackened eyes. But it was as if the dysfunction of the situation didn't even faze him as Dirty grinned at me and said, "Hello, Mrs. Hawkins."

# CHAPTER ELEVEN

# Rocky, Brat, and the Sisterhood

As Dirty Dan's ol' lady—and now wife—I worked at a variety of strip clubs, peep shows, and other such establishments to earn money for him. Although the Vagrants associated with the owners and managers of many of these operations, the only place they owned outright was the Paradise Garden Massage Parlor. And it was here, more than any other place, that the bonds of sisterhood grew among us ol' ladies.

The Paradise Garden Massage Parlor was located in a professional area of downtown Louisville that was known in the 1970s for its hippies, musicians, and artists. It was a three-story cinder-block building with an orange fire escape that ran up the front of the building. In the back was plenty of parking off the street so the customers could hide their cars. The front office was complete with bulletproof glass and an intercom system that connected throughout the entire building to sound the alarm in case of a raid. The intercom also allowed the manager to ensure that the customers weren't hurting the women working there and that the women were handing over all the money they earned.

The Paradise Garden was a legitimately licensed massage parlor even though much more than massages took place on the second and third floors of the building. During this time in the city of Louisville, all the women working there had to have a massage license through the proper channels so the police knew who was operating within such establishments. Before we could get our licenses, we had to be screened by the health department for any venereal diseases and receive documentation that we were clean.

Of course, because of the illegal activities that took place there daily, the Vagrants avoided having their names on anything legal concerning the massage parlor. Instead, they put everything under the name of the parlor's manager, Rocky, who was an ol' lady like me and barely twenty-one years old. Rocky was tasked with not only making the parlor as profitable as the Vagrants desired, but also keeping herself and all of us who worked there safe from police raids.

Therefore, a careful system was set up to ensure the police never caught us doing more than giving massages. Men had to show ID to be let through the steel doors on the first floor, and an index file kept track of returning customers who were safe to solicit for prostitution. Once inside, the men paid twenty to fifty dollars (depending on the length of the massage they wanted) and then went to the sitting room, where Rocky would have the girls line up so they could select who they wanted.

The woman would then lead the man upstairs and have him undress in what used to be a working steam room, put on a towel, and then place his clothes in a locker room. The massage rooms were all small, with concrete walls and windows that were never open, so that it was always musty and stale inside. The rooms contained a massage table, baby powder, baby oil, alcohol for the massages, and a timer the women set based on which service the men paid for.

After the massage, the woman asked the customer if he wanted anything else—or in my case, I would often say, "For twenty more dollars, we can talk about it." And for the most part, that's what I would do—talk about it. I stashed the money in my pocket and received my fifty percent from the house, all without having to have sex. However, if that customer returned, he knew not to choose me again because he would get conned for his money.

If it was one of the other ol' ladies, she might invite the customer up to the third floor, where there was a larger room that contained a full-size waterbed. Rocky had to unlock this room with a key, as it locked automatically whenever you entered or exited. Customers paid extra money to go to this room with the girl of their choice.

It wasn't that I never went into this room with a customer, because I did; I just remembered my mother's words about going to jail and the terrible things that would happen to me there. So I saw every customer as a potential undercover policeman and lived in a constant state of fear that soliciting prostitution would land me behind bars like so many of my brothers.

Because I avoided prostituting as much as I could, I earned far less than the other ol' ladies. Returning customers avoided me, and I didn't earn the big money you got for going to the third floor. And Dirty Dan, of course, never failed to notice.

One night, I went to the clubhouse between working at the massage parlor all day and the bars later that night. I hadn't made any money, because there had been no business that day, least of all for a girl who was known to trick men out of their money. As soon as I walked inside, Dirty met me at the door by the pool table in the front room. Most of the brothers were standing at the bar in the adjacent room.

"Did you make any money, Brat?"

Knowing the tone of his voice meant I was in trouble, I reluctantly said, "No."

Before I could get another word out, Dirty punched me in the face so hard that my frail little body flew over the length of the pool table. I landed on the other side, and one of my boots slid off my foot. In a panic, I jumped to my feet and ran back and forth around the pool table, hobbling on one boot in my attempt to stay away from this towering six-foot-tall man. I cried and begged Dirty not to hit me again as I promised to bring home money the next day.

Finally, he relented, but still, within minutes, both of my eyes were blackened from just one punch. On one side of my face, the bruise extended beyond my hairline. Now I really couldn't make money; no one wanted a girl who looked like this.

The next day, I was sent back to work in spite of my injury. Rocky, the manager of the Paradise Garden, sent me to the local drugstore to pick up supplies for the massage parlor. She did this often just to give me something to do while everyone else was busy making money. I hung my head in shame and dragged my feet as I headed toward the drugstore. This was all I was good for—all I was anymore: a slave sent out to purchase lotion, baby powder, and dozens of condoms for a whorehouse. I could only imagine what the store clerk thought of me when I told him I was there to pick up the order for the Paradise Garden Massage Parlor.

Once I had picked up my order, I went back to watching my feet drag across the sidewalk on my journey back to the

Paradise Garden. Then I heard a familiar voice call out my name. Looking up for the first time, I followed the voice and saw that it belonged to my mother.

"Mary!" she said. "Oh my God, Mary, what happened?"

Her eyes fixed on the bruises on my face, she reached out to me, but I turned away without a word. I refused to look at the woman I had begged to love me, not because I didn't need her, but because of the shame of the person I had become. I couldn't look at her or tell her why I had been beaten or what I was doing on the street right now. So I pulled away even as she continued reaching out for me and calling after me. Eventually, she stopped in the middle of the street and just watched me as I kept walking, never saying a word and keeping my shame to myself.

Even though I was too ashamed to tell my own mother about my life at the massage parlor, I had a host of other motherly figures in the other ol' ladies who worked at the Paradise Garden with me. Jabbering Jackie was one such sister. She was a few decades older than I was and understood the Vagrants and their ways better than many.

One night, after a long night at the massage parlor, Jackie and I came back to another house owned by the Vagrants just a few doors down from the clubhouse. While we had been working, the brothers spent their time smoking, drinking, and doing drugs, making the main room as filthy as ever. Before we went to sleep, Jackie started to dust off the coffee table and dump out some ashtrays, but her ol' man pulled out a pistol and shot at the table right next to where she was cleaning, nearly blowing off her hand in the process.

"Sit your a—— down, woman," he barked. "This is a party."

The brothers thought this was hilarious, but Jackie and I decided to retreat to the next room, where a large bed was calling our name after a long day of work. The rooms were separated only by a pair of French doors, so we struggled to fall asleep amid the brothers' music and raucous laughter less than twenty feet away.

Meanwhile, Dirty decided he wanted to play with the gun so he could impress his brothers even more than Jabbering Jackie's ol' man. So as we were drifting off to sleep in the next room, Dirty stood up and shot through the doorway toward the headboard of the bed. The bullets went straight through the headboard just inches above us and buried themselves in the wall. I screamed and clung to Jackie for protection. She held me tight and whispered, "It's okay, baby, just lie still and keep your head down. Don't say anything; just lie still."

The wood from the headboard rained down on us as Dirty shot several times over our heads. He laughed and shouted, "You c——s asleep?" Everyone in the next room cackled while we lay cowering in fear. I don't remember anything after that but lying there and trying to fall asleep, for it was normal to undergo such abuse for their entertainment.

Like the Vagrant brothers, the sisters had a strange but deep connection forged by our time in the trenches together. Although we saw each other through the hardest of times—beatings from our ol' men and nasty encounters with customers—most of us didn't even know each other's real names. Instead, we called each other "sister" while our ol' men referred to us as "c——s" or gave us numbers as if we were cattle.

Many of us, both men and women, also had nicknames that were unique to our character or some event in our lives. I was called Brat because I was one of the smallest, youngest, and most stubborn among the ol' ladies. Rocky, on the other hand, earned her nickname for the darkest of reasons.

Rocky came to the Vagrants through her first ol' man, Tank, who started as a probate back when the club was in Butchertown on my friend Angie's street. Eventually, Tank became a full-fledged member and sold off Rocky to a cruel man named Mad Dog. The Vagrants passed ol' ladies around like pieces of real estate or stocks on the market. The more money an ol' lady made, the higher the price she would bring if she was sold among them. And if you wanted to leave? You had to buy yourself out. So if your record of turning tricks deemed you valuable among the Vagrants, this actually put your life in greater danger than if you didn't make much money, because the Vagrants wanted to make sure their top income earners continued to be profitable for them.

I couldn't be sold because no one wanted me (thank God). I was hard to break and had to be forced through beatings and threats to turn tricks. On the other hand, Rocky was too valuable to be sold. She did as she was told and made a lot of money for her ol' man. And to my measureless benefit, she used her influence to protect me as much as she could by finding chores for me to do at the massage parlor while all the other ol' ladies were prostituting.

I didn't realize just how much Rocky did for me until she didn't show up to work one day. Or the next. Or the one after that. In her absence, both the safety and the profitability of the parlor started dipping. I was forced to take on many of her responsibilities, but since I did not know how to read or keep books, profits were plunging.

The Vagrants didn't care that Rocky was gone or that I had no idea how to fill her shoes; they still expected to receive the stacks of cash they had grown accustomed to. Before, Rocky had managed to hide my uselessness with the little errands she had me run. But now that she was gone, I was working double shifts every day, and the Vagrants were noticing that I was a weak link in the chain. I thought I would go crazy if I didn't get a break from those concrete walls, but as with every other matter with the Vagrants, there was no escape.

Although everyone avoided talking about why Rocky was absent, I heard she had been in the hospital at some point. Still, with each passing day, both my stress and my anger at her rose. The Vagrants were breathing down my neck, and I was terrified by the knowledge that if the parlor were raided, I was now the one who would take the fall. How could Rocky abandon me like this? Every day I lived in fear of the police taking me to jail or the Vagrants giving me the beating of my life for failing to bring in money, and yet she was off somewhere taking her sweet time getting back to work.

Finally, after about a month of this, Dirty Dan told me Rocky was back. I flew downstairs, ready to give her a piece of my mind for leaving me for so long.

Nothing could have prepared me for what I found.

Rocky's eyes were totally bloodshot—not a speck of white in them, like something out of a horror movie. Her entire face was multiple colors, her jaw was wired shut, and her throat had fresh scars from where the doctors had cut into it for reconstructive surgery. On top of that, she was fifteen pounds lighter and looked as if she hadn't been able to move for weeks.

The story Rocky told the police was that she had been mugged. But the police knew better. No one got such a violent beating from being robbed. No, Rocky's beating was a matter of personal vengeance.

It turned out that Rocky hadn't been transferred from Tank, her first ol' man, to Mad Dog as peaceably as I had once thought. Rocky had left Tank, and he swore to make her pay if she ever got with another brother. Sometime later, Dirty Dan had found Rocky at a bar and drew her back into the Vagrants by giving her to Mad Dog.

Tank was furious, but he bided his time until one night, there was another national party being held at the Louisville clubhouse. Like everyone else, Rocky was drunk and high, and she wasn't thinking about Tank's desire for vengeance. For their part, the brothers were celebrating by taking turns having sex with the same woman in one of the upstairs bedrooms. This left Rocky and Tank alone downstairs.

"Do you know where your new ol' man is?" Tank asked her.

"No," she said.

"He's upstairs with the rest of them with that train c——."

Rocky was hurt, and Tank began to tell her that since Mad Dog was upstairs cheating on her, it was only fair that she could have sex with him, her first ol' man. Her defenses lowered, Rocky agreed.

However, Mad Dog did not think it "fair" that Rocky would have sex with another man, even if it was her former ol' man. When Mad Dog caught them, he began to beat Rocky—beat her and beat her again and again all through the night. When he got tired, he would take a break and then come back again with renewed strength. As always, the other brothers watched like it was one of their pit bull fights. The ol' ladies who witnessed it were threatened with the same treatment if they told anyone. That was why I never found out, because I had been working the night shift at one bar or another while all this was going on.

Mad Dog beat Rocky to the point of unconsciousness and then packed her nostrils with cocaine to dull the pain. Then he kept her locked in the house for three days without medical attention. Rocky was blinded from the swelling in her eyes, but she eventually crawled and felt her way out of the house. The neighbors heard her calling out for help and drove her to the hospital, where she remained for weeks. The brothers visited her regularly—but only to ensure she didn't spill all she knew to the police.

The very day she was released from the hospital, Rocky went back to work at the Paradise Garden. She remained with Mad Dog, and no one ever spoke of the beating again—except that now everyone called her "Rocky" because after her beating, she looked worse than Rocky Balboa after fifteen rounds of boxing at the end of *Rocky I*.

Needless to say, I was horrified and felt like scum for ever having been upset with Rocky. I was beyond relieved to pass management of the massage parlor back to her, and I began to watch my mouth a little more. After all, if the Vagrants were willing to do something like that to one of their most valuable ol' ladies, what would they do to an uncooperative kid like me?

Rocky wasn't the only top earner to have her life threatened. Velvet was another ol' lady whom the Vagrants exploited like the slave she was. For several years, she worked around the clock six days a week. No matter how much she brought home from both shifts, it was never enough. Her only relief was Sundays, when the Vagrants had what they called the "Sunday run"—a day when the entire club got together and hung out at the local bars or some event in the city to show off their bikes and flex their muscles as the baddest bikers in town.

But outside of Sunday, Velvet and the rest of us ol' ladies were forced to work every day from eleven in the morning at the massage parlor until the bars shut down in the early hours of the morning. But it was worse for Velvet because she consistently brought in more money than almost any other ol' lady. And the more money she made, the more she was expected to make the next day. There were no sick days or skipped shifts for her—not when her ol' man became accustomed to the wads of cash she brought home.

When she joined the Vagrants, Velvet was beautiful, intelligent, and bright, but as the years passed, she became drained, battered, and broken. Then one day she disappeared. This wasn't unheard of; women often got passed around or dumped when they were no longer of use. But Velvet was still in her prime, and no one seemed to know what happened to her.

It wasn't until decades later that Rocky revealed a secret to me that she had carried with her for fear of what her crime would cost her. After watching Velvet being beaten and worked to death, Rocky finally couldn't stand it any longer and bought her a bus ticket to California, where her family was from. Rocky took her to the bus station early one morning and never breathed a word of it to anyone, because both Velvet's ol' man and Rocky's would be sure to go after Rocky for helping a top earner escape. We never heard from Velvet again but hoped that she found a more peaceful life than the one she had left behind.

Of course, it wasn't just the bad times that bonded us together as sisters. There were good times too, like when a group of us went to a Bob Seger concert and got invited backstage. We had dressed our best, with all the jewelry and fine clothes that came with being the stars our pimps had groomed us to be.

Outside of the clubhouse and the red light district, we were just a group of pretty, giggling young women enjoying a concert, and we caught the eye of the young roadies who traveled with the band. They lifted us over the gates and gave us backstage passes that we stuck onto the legs of our blue jeans. Then we spent the whole night taking pictures and receiving guitar picks from the band.

No one knew who we were or what we did outside that concert, and the roadies treated us with respect, like we were real ladies—something we weren't accustomed to. Of course, once we got back to the clubhouse and showed off all our trophies, our ol' men accused us of sleeping with the roadies, but not even they could dampen our spirits.

The sisters played pranks on each other too—but not the nasty and evil kind that the brothers pulled on us and each other. One day at the massage parlor, the sisters taught me how to eat lobster. Afterward, they convinced me that if I buried the shell, it would bring me good luck. So, high as I was on some brain-altering chemical, I went outside and began burying the lobster shell while the girls stood there laughing at me. I wasn't satisfied with my first burial site, so I ended up digging it up and reburying it three more times until dirt was all over my outfit and under my fingernails. Needless to say, that was another slow day for me as far as clients were concerned.

As close as all of us sisters were, many of us lost touch as the years went by. We lived in such a violent and drug-infested culture that few lived to see their fifties, as I have. The rest moved around so often that, like Velvet, it became hard to track any of them down.

Rocky and I lost touch for almost thirty years until we found each other again in 2012. Seeing her again was like finding an old comrade-in-arms. This was the woman who had taught me how to drive, how to coordinate outfits, how to clean up after myself—all the things a big sister would have done if I'd lived another life. If I ever had a problem or just wanted to cry, she listened. She was there for me and protected me even when I had nothing to offer her in return. I thank God every day that we survived all that we did so we can sit across the table from each other, now two *actual* old ladies, and reminisce about the sisterhood that saw us through our darkest of days.

# CHAPTER TWELVE

# Police Run-Ins
# and the Last Straw

My eighteenth birthday came and went without much excitement. The real milestone I was waiting for was turning twenty, when it would finally be legal for me to work in the bars and strip clubs I had been working in since I was sixteen. Until then, the name on my fake ID, along with my stage names, was my lifeline and protection against my childhood terror of the legal system.

In the fall of 1978, the police were cracking down on prostitution and underage girls working on the strip. They knew I was one of those girls, but as long as I could pull off the lie that I was the twenty-three-year-old woman on that ID, they couldn't do anything. Dirty had drilled me to memorize all of her information so that I could rattle off her name, age, and Social Security number no matter how drunk or high I was. To this day, I can still tell you her entire name, first, middle, and last.

But that all came to an end when I was working at Sensations, a strip club next door to Baby Dolls, where I had gotten my start as a dancer. Like the manager of Baby Dolls, the manager of Sensations knew I was underage. I had been working for him since I was seventeen, and even though he had just gotten out of prison himself, I trusted him to protect me from going to jail.

The morning everything went wrong, the manager asked me to put my ID in the club's safe. I was forever losing my purse and my money, so I had every reason to believe him when he said it was for safe keeping.

A few hours later, the police came into the bar and demanded to see everyone's ID. As always, my heart started pounding at the sight of those uniforms, but I knew what to do. I went straight to the manager and asked for my ID out of the safe.

But for some reason, he refused. Actually, he just ignored me as if I hadn't spoken. I couldn't believe it. He was the only one who had keys to the safe, and without him, the police were going to take me away.

The manager's betrayal didn't stop there. He let the police believe that the bartender was the manager, and since the police held managers responsible for hiring underage girls, it was off to jail with both of us. The police didn't do anything so dramatic as handcuff us, but when they told us it was time to go, the bartender tested their generosity by saying she wanted to finish eating her pie first. I couldn't believe her nerve. I was nearly hysterical at the thought of being hauled away in a police car, and here she was calmly eating her pie. *I guess you don't get pie in jail*, I thought.

I found out later that the manager had purposely set me up to be arrested that day. I think as part of staying out of prison himself, he agreed to help the police in their raids on underage workers. He knew my ID was fake, and he took advantage of my naïveté by asking to hold my ID so the police would finally be able to nail me. It wasn't the first or last time I learned the hard way that people are willing to take advantage of you to better themselves.

The car ride to the jail was every bit as awful as the night the police had taken me away from my boyfriend Ray. But instead of going to the Children's Center, I was going to jail. Jail. Just like my mother had always taunted me, I would be behind bars rather than outside of them visiting one of my brothers. Trapped with nowhere else to go.

But the saddest part of all was that when I got to jail, I found that I wasn't the only member of my family to be arrested that evening. I had yet to give the police my real name, so they sent me to wait in a line until they could process me. As I waited, I turned around and there was one of my brothers, waiting to be processed himself.

"Mary!" he said, shocked. "What are you in for?"

"They caught me in the bar," I said, barely able to get the words out.

We both were so ashamed for each other. I looked like the hooker that I was, and he looked like the poor boy who robbed places so he could get something to eat. The coincidence made me sick. I was so ashamed of myself. I couldn't help but think I should have stayed at home and taken care of my brother. Instead, here I was wearing too much makeup, a dress that was way too short, and spiked heels that said everything about who I actually was.

When I sat down to be processed by the arresting officer, another officer noticed me and stopped in his tracks.

"Mary? What are you doing here?"

It was Rob, a man I had known from childhood, when I lived with Angie next door to the Vagrants' old clubhouse. As I began to explain what had happened, the arresting officer blurted out, "I knew you weren't twenty-three!" He turned to Rob. "Tell me who she really is."

The two of them stepped aside to talk, leaving me to wonder how this new development would impact my fate. After a few long minutes, Rob came back and said, "Listen, Mary, I'll get you out of this. I'll tell the judge you were helping me."

I should have known Rob was doing me an incredible favor, but in the world I had come from, the worst thing anyone could accuse you of was being a snitch. It was better to take the fall all by yourself than ever appear to be in league with the authorities. Or so the Vagrants had taught me. So even though it was against my own self-interest, I said, "I don't want your help."

He sighed impatiently. "Fine. Then go over there and tell the man who you are and who you're not, or I'm going to. But if I do it, you'll be charged with giving false information, and that's a hell of a lot worse charge."

Now even more terrified, I returned to the arresting officer and told him the truth. He put me in a cell with four other girls, where I spent hours too scared even to move or speak. Eventually, I was released on my own recognizance without having to pay for bail. A court date was set for one month later.

I cried through the whole month waiting on my court date. I obsessed over and over about going to prison; I'm sure my subconscious was taking me back to when my mother had tormented me after getting caught with my childhood love. Dirty Dan tried to comfort me through my tears and made certain I had a lawyer for court.

The court date came and went, and the charge ended up being nothing more than underage drinking in a bar. I paid a small fine, and the whole thing was dismissed. But for me, it was a nightmare. I was sure something worse would happen—

if not that day, then sometime down the road, and I would be just like all my brothers, spending my best years in a cage.

After the ordeal, the arresting officer took me aside and said, as kindly as possible, "Listen, if you really want to work in the business, just go where you can do it legally at eighteen years old. You're too young for the bars."

That was the first time an adult had given me any advice about working in the bars, and I took it for all it was worth. I did everything I could to obey the law. I did not return to a strip club until I was of legal age to be a dancer. In fact, I went personally to the Alcohol and Beverage Control Board and asked how old one had to be to work in the strip clubs. They told me twenty and a day. So for the next two years, I refused to work anywhere but the massage parlor and the peep shows.

The peep shows were the nastiest places to work. They were located in the back of a triple-X store, where—similar to the picture booths I had worked in—there was a line of small, private booths where customers could watch women dance and make sexually explicit poses on a small stage. However, unlike at the picture booths, a window separated me from the customers. I would sit onstage eight hours a day, six days a week, waiting for a man to come in and drop two quarters into the slot. Then music would play and the lights would come on, allowing him to see me while he remained in the dark. Then, when his time was up, the lights would reverse so I could see him but he couldn't see me.

The things I witnessed when those lights came on were straight from hell. Everything imaginable went on inside those booths, where men thought they were safe in the dark. They would masturbate all over the floor, or if more than one man came in together, I could count on seeing them doing some sort of sex act with each other that made my stomach churn.

To try to hold on to my sanity, I began allowing my mind to disassociate from what was going on around me—though there was only so much I could do to protect myself in such a place. Strange how there is often no sanity where there is no sanitation.

When your shift was over, you were expected to lock your booths so management could count the money the next day. You received fifty percent of the quarters that were dropped, if you weren't cheated out of your money. Some of the girls were smart enough to keep count of their drops by keeping tally marks on paper. (I, however, couldn't keep count of my thoughts, let alone my drops.) Next to the window was a hole drilled in the wall where the customers could roll up dollar bills and shove them through to the dancer. Men would often stick their tongues through the hole—another nasty thing we had to witness.

To lock up the booths, you had to walk through semen left by eight hours of customers masturbating inside. I remember tiptoeing in my boots, as they would stick to the floor if you walked normally. The back of the triple-X store was lit only by black lights, and when the music in my booth wasn't on, I could hear the sounds of women moaning and porno music playing in the movie booths. Some poor janitor was paid to mop out the booths once every twenty-four hours, but in this place of no sunlight and no windows, nothing could get rid of the odor of compounded human excretion, which reminded me quite literally of the smell of death.

To leave that environment and attempt to lead a normal life was impossible. Often I felt spacey and way out of touch with reality. Walking out through the store, I tried not to see the assorted sex toys and magazines, and I tried to avoid the strange and creepy people who loitered there, including the male and female prostitutes who had only one thing on their minds.

My single relief was that one of the triple-X stores had the arcade game Space Invaders. I would longingly wait for my break times so I could go play. It was the only normal thing for a teenager to do in a place like that. There were just two ends of the spectrum: Either you became warped while you tried to find a sense of normalcy, or you tried to feel nothing at all so you could survive mentally and emotionally. And all the while, the same smell and spirit of decay hung in the air, and it seemed impossible to wash away no matter how hard I tried.

*

As disgusting as the peep shows were, they at least never brought me legal troubles. Of course, when I wasn't working there, I was at the Paradise Garden with Rocky and the other ol' ladies. I had gotten away with refusing to work in the strip clubs until I was of age, but because of the illegal activities that went on at the massage parlor, I was never free from the fear of prison. And little did I know just how close I came to my fears becoming reality.

By the time I was eighteen, Dirty and I were living in a house out in the country, away from the clubhouse and all of its nastiness. Although I liked living in the country, we had no running water, and our only source of heat was the fireplace. Plus, we were isolated from most people, including my family, so the only time I saw people other than Dirty was at the massage parlor after the long drive into town.

One day I was sitting in the living room waiting for Dirty to take me to work. Although he was sober, Dirty was in one of his moods, and I couldn't put my finger on what the problem was. I could feel his anger building while I quietly sat at the coffee table looking over nude pictures of myself from years before at the picture booth. They had been taken by a regular customer, who had given them to me for some reason.

As I looked over these pictures of my young, exposed body, my shame began to build almost at the same pace as Dirty's mysterious anger. Finally, I tore up one picture and threw the pieces back on the coffee table. Dirty came in from pacing outside and sat down on the couch. I wondered if he might finally be calming down, but then he noticed the torn picture.

Without warning, he lunged at me and began shaking me, and then threw me to the floor in a rage.

I scrambled to my feet and ran outside. "Please don't hurt me, Dirty," I begged, walking backward with my hands up. "I won't do it again."

Dirty ran out after me and bellowed, "You worthless c——! Can't turn a trick, can't make money. You're the sorriest ol' lady I have ever had."

Dirty stalked toward me, and I knew I had nowhere to go. No one could help me in the middle of the country. Then he stopped next to a tree trunk that someone had dug up several weeks before. Although the tree trunk was as big as he was, Dirty—fueled by his irrational anger—grabbed it, lifted it over his head, and threw it at me. I ducked just in time, and it flew over my head.

Dirty managed to grab me again and dragged me by the hair into his truck. He drove us to Louisville, practically shaking with anger while I shook with fear. I was supposed to be going to the Paradise Garden, but instead, he took us to the club-house. When we arrived, he pulled me out of the truck and made me stand in front of the brothers while he shouted that I was to leave and he didn't want me any longer.

It was like Bowling Green all over again. I left in tears and confusion, not understanding why a torn-up picture had almost cost me my life.

That night on the news, I heard that the authorities had raided every massage parlor in Louisville. As the Vagrants had always planned, Rocky took the fall and went to jail while all the brothers remained blameless. Although none of the men went to jail, the massage parlor was facing unprecedented legal scrutiny.

Now I understood the real reason behind Dirty's rage. Sure, he probably hadn't wanted me to rip up the picture; but even more importantly, he had known the raids were happening, and I was the unfortunate soul who happened to be closest when he was expressing his frustration. And in his own twisted way, Dirty had saved me from jail when so many of my sisters had not been as lucky.

Not long after that terrible night, Dirty called me at my mother's house and told me to come home. I did as I was told.

Although Dirty had saved me that time from arrest, he and his stupidity would cause yet another legal entanglement. Across the street from the massage parlor was a pawn shop that was selling a nine-millimeter German pistol—the same kind Dirty had used to shoot at me and Jabbering Jackie. Dirty thought the gun was cool, so he ordered me to make payments on it when I went to work. Nearly every day, I took my measly earnings from the massage parlor and ran across the street to give the owner money until finally the gun was Dirty's.

He was so excited about that gun that he wanted to show it off to everyone. First, we went to the clubhouse, and then we started walking down the street to Mad Dog's house (Rocky's ol' man). Dirty was so proud that he carried the gun in his hand, not bothering to conceal it.

When we got to Mad Dog's porch, suddenly a man yelled

out to us from a car on the street. We turned around and saw that it was an undercover patrol car. Familiar anxiety started to rise up in me as the officer ordered Dirty to come to his car.

"Go inside, Brat," Dirty said, and then pressed the gun into my hands.

I hurried into the house and shoved the gun into a laundry basket full of clothes. Just as I finished burying it, the policeman knocked on the door and said he wanted to talk to me.

"Where's the gun he handed you?" he asked.

"What gun?" I answered.

"I saw you take a gun in the house after he handed it to you."

By now, Dirty was in the back of the patrol car.

"No, that was a pack of cigarettes," I replied. The cop didn't look like he believed me, and I was getting nervous talking to him all by myself. "Look, if you want me to ask him if he has a gun, I will," I said.

"So ask him." He led me to the back of the patrol car and put me inside with Dirty.

"Dirty, he wants the gun," I said.

"Brat, don't give that b——d the gun. I just paid five hundred dollars for it." I wanted to protest, but he cut me off. "Now get out of the car and don't give him s——."

So I knocked on the window and motioned for the officer to let me out. He did so and asked, "Now are you going inside after the gun?"

Trying to keep my voice steady, I said, "He said he doesn't have a gun."

At that point, the officer spun me around and pushed my face into the patrol car. As he placed handcuffs on me, he said, "I can't believe you would protect that piece of s——."

The officer took us both to the precinct to process, and I

was the only one who had handcuffs on. I couldn't believe that I—the skinny little eighteen-year-old girl—was in handcuffs while Dirty—the big, burly owner of the gun—was not. We were charged with having a concealed deadly weapon, but there was no gun entered into evidence. As when I was arrested at the strip club, we were released after not too long, but the toll that being back in jail had on my spirit couldn't be measured.

Again I cried until our court date came. Dirty would hold me and tell me that I wasn't going anywhere and that he wouldn't let them take me. I knew this man had some empathy within him, if only a tiny bit, but never in front of his brothers. The court day came, and our lawyer said the policeman had made a mistake by arresting us and making the charge of concealed deadly weapon without having a weapon for evidence.

Dirty laughed at the policeman and told me we could take his badge if we wanted to. But far from laughing, I felt sick to my stomach. I couldn't bring myself to lie in court or go to trial and say I had no gun when we did. However, before it got to that point, I begged Dirty to plead guilty and admit that there had been probable cause for arrest, and then the judge dismissed the whole thing without charging us with a fine or jail time.

I could breathe easy once again. I promised myself that I would never do anything to get into trouble again, even though it was seeming harder and harder to do so with the Vagrants around.

Dirty and I continued to live in the country. My nineteenth birthday came and went, but everything else remained the same. I still worked around the clock and got nothing but beatings in return.

I didn't realize how close I was to my breaking point until Dirty's sister and her two young children came to stay with us. She was leaving her husband and their middle-class suburban existence out in Rock Springs, Wyoming. Dirty invited her to stay with us while she got back on her feet, but he made it sound like we were living in a nice farm or ranch house, not a rundown place with no water or heat.

My heart broke as I watched Dirty's sister take a job as a waitress at the bar down the street from the Vagrants' clubhouse. She had uprooted her life to live among Vagrants with her children, and even I knew it was not something a mother would choose for her children had she known more. She was now stuck in Louisville with two sweet children who had never before seen such conditions.

That winter, it was so cold that we all had to move into a trailer where we could have water, heat, and electricity. We struggled to make ends meet, but Dirty's sister kept everything afloat for her children. Everything was going well for a while until Dirty went out of town and we ran out of propane for heat. After living in the bitter cold for days without help, Dirty's sister said to me, "I'm leaving and going back to Wyoming. Do you want to come with me?"

It was as if my very brain was numb, and I agreed to go without giving it hardly any thought. After Dirty had dragged me to the National Meet in North Carolina, I had promised myself I would never leave Louisville again, but I was so tired of Dirty's abuse and the misery of my day-to-day existence that I chose to leave with her that very week. She, her children, and I all piled into a Ford Pinto, which made the trip out west nearly as miserable as the summer of '77 on the back of Dirty's chopper.

Along the way, we stopped in New Mexico to visit their

mother. This was the first time I had met my mother-in-law. She was a Christian woman who was kind to me and who tucked me in at night just like she did her grandchildren. I did not share with her that her son was a pimp, but her daughter did and would tell her how worthless Dirty had turned out to be. We stayed for a short time, and I was excited to eat new foods and learn a new culture.

But soon it was time to head out for Rock Springs, Wyoming, where months earlier Dirty's sister had left her husband. Once we reached Rock Springs, within days she found me a job as a waitress. I couldn't bring myself to tell her that I couldn't read or write well enough and didn't have the confidence to work any place where you needed common sense and social skills. And it felt all too familiar having her tell me I had to go to work at someplace I couldn't handle and didn't want to be. I had spent the last three years having a miserable work life laid out for me, and now here I was doing it all over again—this time hundreds of miles away from everything I knew.

The weight of my impulsive decision began to crash down on me. Not long at all after I had arrived, I called my mother and cried that I wanted to come home. My stepfather, Tucker, wired me the money to purchase a Greyhound bus ticket to return to Louisville. I was so nervous about traveling by myself since I knew I would have to transfer several times, and I was worried I would get lost out west somewhere. But I had gone back on my promise to myself never to leave Louisville again, and I was determined to make it right.

Before I left, Dirty's sister told me, "You'll go back to him."

"No, I won't," I answered.

"Yes, you will. You'll go back."

I made another promise to myself that day that I wasn't

going back to Dirty. It wasn't because of any one thing he had done to me, but because I was so stubborn and wanted to keep my word to myself.

So I made the choice not to return to my first pimp, but once back in Louisville, I found that the sex industry was not so easy to leave behind.

# CHAPTER THIRTEEN

# No Longer a Vagrant

When I got home, I moved back in with my mother, stepfather, and some adult brothers, who all lived in a four-room shotgun house. I also went back to working the night shift at the peep shows. I was counting down the days until I turned twenty and a day so I could work in the bars and wouldn't have to witness the perversion that took place at the peep shows.

Just as before, I helped Tucker with the bills and provided for everyone's needs even as they did drugs and never worked themselves. Whenever someone asked me for money, I gave it away freely because I felt guilty for how I earned it. I was so accustomed to handing it over, I didn't think it was mine.

Everyone around me had drug or alcohol problems, but I stayed away from all of it since I had been tortured by others' addictions when I was a child. However, even though I was rarely drunk or high, I had my own issues. Because I worked all night, I slept during the day, but that sleep was never easy or restful. I often woke up in tears and screaming at the top of my lungs. I didn't know why; I was free now, and no one could hurt me. I should have been at peace.

But the demons were reminding me of where I had been.

The things I attempted to forget or pretended didn't happen came alive in my sleep. Laughing evil faces flashed in and out of my dreams, and I was constantly running from them but getting nowhere as they chased me. The same dream plagued me for years. Even in a house full of addicts, it was embarrassing to wake up crying out so loudly that it drew everyone's attention.

Tucker said once after one of my episodes, "We have to get that girl some psychiatric help."

My mother replied from the next room, "There is nothing wrong with that b——."

I was so ashamed of myself. Normal people don't wake from their sleep screaming because demons were chasing them. I worried that I was becoming mentally unstable, but what could I do but continue to work and survive as I always had?

I was lonely too, but this time, no matter how many times Dirty literally rode his bike into my mother's living room to impress everyone, I held him at arm's length even as the rest of my family fawned over him. Mama cooked for him and he called her "Ma," and she liked all the attention he gave her. He bragged that my mother had given me to him and that I was a second-generation ol' lady since my aunt had also been with the Vagrants in the 1960s.

He seemed to charm everyone except me, because I knew what he was and what he had done to me. My mother must have known too, especially after the day she saw me outside the massage parlor with two black eyes. In fact, everyone in that house knew he had beaten me, but he flattered them all so much that the truth didn't seem to matter.

After a while, Dirty gave up on the idea that I would make a good ol' lady. He called me one day and told me he wanted a divorce so he could begin to see the former ol' lady of another

Vagrant, who made him a lot of money. Although I no longer wanted anything to do with Dirty, that phone call still hurt. It wasn't because I loved him; rather, it was the fact that I was being divorced by a pimp. I was so useless that even a Vagrant didn't want me. Even though I had left him—a pimp who purchased, traded, and sold women—he had found a way to reject me. Everyone—including me—viewed me as a whore and nothing more. Yet through it all, I still held tight to the dream that someday I would be more than what I had come to be.

Dirty wasn't the only Vagrant I had to worry about. Whenever one of the brothers saw me downtown coming to or leaving the peep show, they told me I couldn't work unless I gave the Vagrants a cut of my money. After all, ol' ladies were slaves who were expected to pay for their freedom if they left the club. So I tried hard to stay out of sight when I worked in the red light district. Yes, even down in the pit, I had to skirt around and hide like a criminal.

Eventually, the club president told the Vagrants to leave me alone and allow me to work. I think he knew I was just trying to survive. He had known of me as the street rat who stayed with my friend next door to the clubhouse and knew how hard my childhood had been. So I was left alone to work the peep shows without buying myself out, like so many other girls who were expected to pay for their freedom.

And although I was free in many ways, I was now alone in the red light district with no protection from the sharks in the streets. No one would have dared touch me while I was Dirty Dan's ol' lady, but now I didn't have his threatening presence to ward off those who would victimize me. But I told myself I could survive; after all, I had done everything on my own since I was four years old. And someday, somebody would love me.

\*

Months after Dirty called for his divorce, I found what I thought was love in one of my peep show booths. Unlike a typical peep show customer, this boy was just a curious teenager whose friend had dragged him there one night. When the lights came on in my side of the booth, I immediately noticed him. He had long, brown locks of curls that hung down to his shoulders, beautiful green eyes, and a smile that caught my attention. He was just a typical teenager in jeans and a T-shirt, but being a typical teenager was all that I wanted right about then.

He and his friend were laughing and giggling like little girls, and after a minute, I hollered out over the music to try to talk to him. He couldn't hear me, so after their time was up and I could see them but they could no longer see me, I turned down the music and tried again.

"What's your name?" I yelled.

"Who, me?" he replied. He appeared to be embarrassed as he looked over at his friend.

"Yeah, you."

"Keith," he replied.

I wanted so badly to meet someone my age who would take me out on a real date—the way teenagers had fun and fell in love. I asked, "Would you want to come back at two in the morning and I'll meet you out front?"

"I guess I can do that, yes."

He was smiling as he said it, and my heart soared. For the first time in years, a boy my age wanted to see me!

The rest of the night went by in a flurry of anticipation and excitement as I waited for two in the morning to come around. When I got a break from the windows flashing off and on, I eagerly applied makeup and dug through my dance bag for something cute to wear. As soon as my shift ended, I hurried to the bathroom to clean up and check my makeup just once more. Excited and bubbly, I stumbled up the stairs leading back to the stage and had to slow down to gather my composure.

So at two in the morning, I met this dreamy teenage boy in front of Flashers. There was nothing remarkable about that first date; we had coffee (which I paid for) and talked for a few hours, and then he drove me home. But to me, who for years had been courted only by a pimp, it meant everything.

Before long, Keith was the boyfriend I had been longing for. I saw him nearly every day as he started picking me up from work and spending a few fun hours with me before dropping me off at my mother's. Right away, my mother didn't like him, because he didn't make eye contact or talk much—very different from Dirty Dan's charming ways. Keith didn't like my family either, and I was ashamed of them because I felt like we were white trash compared to him.

Every time we went out, I always paid for the food, and I also insisted on paying for gas when he drove me back and forth from work. It wasn't that he demanded my money like Dirty Dan had; it was just that he didn't have a job. He was a little younger than I was and still lived with his parents, but I never gave any of it a second thought because I already paid for everything for everybody.

Within months, we moved in together, into a three-room apartment—my first real home. I was in love, and I gladly paid the rent and for all of our expenses. I had done the same thing for Dirty, but it felt so different this time because Keith and I felt more like equals.

But unlike Dirty, Keith deeply disliked me working at

Flashers, where we had met. He hated that I had been a Vagrant's ol' lady and that I still carried Dirty's last name. Because it made him angry, I stopped telling him about my past, but that didn't keep him from throwing what I had already shared with him back in my face and from putting me down in front of friends and family.

The verbal abuse slowly turned into physical abuse as well. I thought only bikers smacked their women, but even though Keith hated everything about Dirty Dan, here he was turning into something of a biker himself.

I didn't know what it was about me that caused this sort of behavior from the people I loved—first my mother, then Dirty, and now Keith. But I thought I deserved it from Keith because of where he had found me. Besides, I was accustomed to people talking to and treating me in a worse manner than what he was dishing out. But the abuse was getting worse as time went by, and although he asked, I refused to marry him and tie myself to another abuser.

Keith's distaste for my work reached a high note when I became pregnant with his child. Even though his abuse and control increased, I was so excited that I hardly noticed. This was the first time I had become pregnant since the child I had conceived while on the road with Dirty Dan, and I vowed to myself that I would be a good mother. I would protect this child and love her and give her the world I never had. And her name would be Sara (which means "princess") because I was going to treat her like the princess she was.

At five months pregnant, I had to stop working in the peep shows because there was no hiding my condition when I was dancing nude. My boss suggested I draw unemployment, which I thought was kind of him. I promised to return once I had my baby and recovered.

Of course, once I arrived at the unemployment office, I had to explain why I had been laid off from my job. So in front of a panel of people, I submitted a claim to show cause for why I had been dismissed from work. I convinced them that my body was my tool and that it was out of commission due to the baby growing inside me. I believe I was the first dancer in Louisville, if not all of Kentucky, who drew unemployment because I was pregnant and thus of no use to the sex industry.

So my baby's father and I waited each week on my unemployment check. Since he still couldn't find work, he had nothing to worry about except controlling me. The verbal and physical harassment continued, and I felt like I couldn't go anywhere or even think without him telling me. My family wasn't any help because they had their own problems (self-inflicted and not); in fact, my mother made everything worse by showing up at our apartment drunk, which seemed to prove Keith's judgment that we were white trash.

Meanwhile, I had this overwhelming feeling—some might call it intuition—that my baby was going to die. As Sara got bigger and bigger by the day, I would tell family members with increasing hysteria that my baby wasn't going to make it. Even as they tried to comfort me, they surely wondered why I would say such a thing, and between that and my screaming nightmares, they probably thought I was going crazy. My mother went one step further when one night, in a drunken stupor, she screamed that she *wished* my baby would die.

My breaking point finally came when I was eight months pregnant. Keith decided that he wanted to go out and that I couldn't go with him. To make sure I couldn't go anywhere without him while he was gone, he pulled out a hammer and nails and started nailing the windows shut. At first, I couldn't believe what was happening, but then I started waddling around after him screaming for him to stop. But he ignored me, and when he was finished, he marched out the front door and slammed it behind him.

Then the hammering started on the door. As I stood on the other side, banging and pleading, the nails started poking through the door as he pounded them into place. No matter how much I cried and begged, he didn't stop until there was a halo of pointy nails surrounding me.

A minute after the hammering stopped, I heard the car start, and then he was gone, leaving me pregnant and alone on the second floor of the apartment building with no clue when he would be back. I slid down the door and sat on the floor while I held my belly and cried. I had no phone and no way to get to the hospital if something went wrong. How long was he going to be gone? What if I went into labor? Was this how my baby was going to die?

I must have fallen asleep replaying these questions in my head because the next thing I knew, it was morning and I was awakened by the sound of Keith pulling the nails out of the door.

The stress of Keith's abuse and my own anxiety was finally taking its toll on my health. Shortly after the nailing incident, the doctor admitted me to the hospital with toxemia (now called preeclampsia). I was to be on complete bed rest until the baby arrived. Since he couldn't do much to control or abuse me while I was in the hospital, Keith didn't visit me very often. Instead, my mother and cousin Dolores came to stay with me. My mother slept on the floor while Dolores kept me company.

One night, at the stroke of midnight, the first labor pain hit me. I called the nurse immediately, and she said it wasn't labor but constipation. I thought to myself, *If this is constipation, I would hate to think what labor is.*

Once the nurse left, my mother got up and said, "She doesn't know what the hell she's talking about. I've had fifteen children, so I know what labor is, and *this* is labor."

She pointed to my belly as it rose up with another contraction.

"What do I do, Mama?" I asked, feeling fear rise inside me. How could I deliver the baby if my mother thought the medical staff couldn't help me? Maybe *this* was how the baby was going to die.

"I can't do anything for you, baby; you just have to go through it."

Then she laid back down and went to sleep.

My cousin Dolores stayed up with me and held my hand, trying to distract me from the pain. At one point, she said, "Mary, look out the window; there's a house on fire. Concentrate on it."

"No!" I said, panicked. "I can't. It's a sign of death, Dolores."

I was in agony all night and exhausted from lack of sleep. At eight o'clock the next morning, the doctor came in to examine me and assured me that I was in fact in labor. However, my blood pressure was also off the charts, and I began to have double vision. I was so tired and delirious from the stress on my body that I hardly knew what was happening. The doctor and nurses swarmed around me, attaching a heart monitor to my stomach and checking my vitals. Even in my stupor, I sensed a note of panic in what was going on. Every labor is intense, but there was something else going on. And still I had no baby and no word about where her father was.

At one point, my mother came to my bedside, grabbed my hand, and said, "Mary, please don't die. You're my baby; please don't die."

*Die?* I thought. *Why would she say that? What's all this talk about death?*

I finally demanded the doctor's attention and managed to gasp out, "Is my baby dead?"

He opened his mouth to speak, but nothing came out. He could only nod his head yes. They had known for several minutes but were trying to keep it from me so as not to upset me further and stress my already-failing heart.

The heart monitor on my belly was silent as they finally removed it. My blood pressure was still skyrocketing, so I was in an odd state of stress and yet numbness as they rushed me from the labor room to the delivery room. It took some time to deliver my baby, and when I finally did, there was no cry.

The nurse wrapped her in a blanket and brought her to me, but I couldn't bear to look at her. I turned my head away as she approached.

"Please take her away," I said. "I don't want to see her."

To this day, I have no idea what my sweet Sara looked like. I can only say that the shock and grief in that moment prevented me from looking at her, stealing that memory forever.

I woke up in recovery to find Keith standing next to my bed crying. I had no comforting words for this man who had abandoned me, and I fell back to sleep. The next time I came to myself, he wasn't there, and everyone else had gone home too. My mother was in shock somewhere, likely guilt-ridden for wishing this fate on her daughter and granddaughter. The nurse told me that my blood pressure was going down, but I was alone again—more alone than I had ever felt now that this baby I had never met was gone forever.

The cruelest thing of all was that the hospital put me on the ward with the other mothers. Whenever feeding time came around, I could hear the babies being wheeled down the hall, crying until they were reunited with their waiting mothers. I saw their cradles and watched them with their happy mothers and fathers before I returned to my bed, alone and without a baby to hold.

The doctors kept me for a few days to recover. After experiencing such a trauma, I didn't think anything of releasing Sara's body to Keith because I trusted that he would take care of the burial. However, I learned later that he refused to allow my family to see her before he laid her to rest, thus tearing away from us any hope of closure.

Several days went by and I hadn't heard from Keith. I called around until I finally got ahold of him at his friend's house. I demanded to know where he had been and why he hadn't been there for me through all of this and why he had treated my family the way he had.

His only response was, "Listen, Mary, I'm with someone else now. I don't want you anymore."

I was too shocked to respond. How could this be? While I had been carrying and then giving birth to our stillborn baby, he had been with another woman. He was jealous of Dirty Dan and watched my every move, but it turned out I should have been the one watching. It was too cruel to fathom.

Even worse, I found out later that Keith actually had been in the hospital while I was in labor, but he had brought his new girlfriend with him. He paraded her in front of my family in the waiting room while Sara was dying and I was fighting for my life. No one had told me so as not to raise my blood pressure further.

It was like a nightmare from which I couldn't wake up. I hadn't even left the hospital yet, and my baby was dead and my boyfriend didn't want me anymore. When I finally was released, I went home to my mother's house with the worst hurt I have ever known to this day.

*

It took me twenty-five years to visit my baby's grave. For many years, I couldn't even bring myself to say her name and instead referred to her as "the baby that died," as if she were an object.

Then one day, one of my sisters spoke up and said, "You gave that girl a name. What's her name?" When I hesitated, she persisted, "Say her name!"

"Sara," I finally said, though it felt like dredging up pain from a soul where no more pain could fit. "Yes, I gave her a name, and it was Sara."

In 2005, I finally went to the graveyard where Sara was buried, and brought along some toys and a statue of a childlike angel. I knew that Keith owned the grave, but I didn't think Sara had a headstone, so I didn't know where to look. I went to the office and asked the attendant, "Can you help me find my daughter's grave? I believe she was buried here in 1980, and I'm not sure if her last name is Thomas or Hawkins. And she was a newborn."

He nodded. "Then she would be in baby heaven. I'll look it up."

Once he found the information, he escorted me through the courtyard and directly behind the chapel. He started counting his steps along a row of statues and stones littered with balloons and toys.

Then he stopped and said, "This should be it."

I thanked him, and then I knelt down and placed the angel statue on the spot. The statue reminded me of the angel who had visited me when I was a child.

"I'm here, baby," I said to that spot of earth. "I'm sorry I left you and forgot you. I'm your mama, and I remember you wiggling inside me. I love you, Sara."

Then I cried for the first time for my baby and for the others I had given back to God before their birth. I cried for the terrible pain I went through that week. I cried until I thought I might not ever be able to stop. Then I prayed, *God, give me strength to rise up from this ground and believe in my heart that someday I will see her sweet spirit in heaven. Amen.*

# CHAPTER FOURTEEN

# Twenty and a Day

When I returned home after Sara's birth, I spent the next several days grieving and not eating. I couldn't imagine moving on with life after this. I couldn't imagine going back to work again, falling in love again, being a mother again. How can any parent move on after losing a baby like that?

It didn't take Keith but a few days to come back around and try to worm his way back in. He didn't even come himself at first—or maybe he thought I wouldn't let him in if he came—so he sent his brother to knock on my mother's front door.

When I answered the door, his brother said, "Keith wants to talk to you. He said he's sorry for what he did. I told him you probably wouldn't have any more to do with him, but he begged me to come and ask you to come back to him."

I wish I had had the strength to turn him away and reject Keith as he had done to me at a time when I needed him the most. But my spirit was broken, and I just wanted to know what I had done to deserve such cruelty. I never got an answer; I just returned thinking I had let him down by losing his child. I always felt I was as low as you could get because I had worked in the sex industry, and any awful thing anyone did to me was deserved.

I went back to Keith out of grief and rejection at a time when I desperately needed someone to love me. For a while, he was good to me as I grieved and cried for months on end. We tried to forget about what he had done to me by not talking about it.

Now that I wasn't working, we moved out of our apartment and into his parents' storage room. This quickly proved to be a mistake because the abuse began again and in fact got worse. I think Keith's guilt and shame over being with a harlot like me was eating him alive, and he was taking it out on me.

Here I was again, desperate and feeling abandoned and rejected. I felt as though I was being rightly punished for my sins. And like every woman who has been with an angry and hurting man, I wanted desperately for him to get better and love me as I had always longed to be loved.

The worst part of the abuse was that he started using Sara's death to hurt me mentally and emotionally. He had taken pictures of her during the viewing at the funeral home, and every once in a while, he pulled them out and tried to force me to look at them. I would close my eyes tightly and try to push him away as he shoved the pictures in my face and tried to pry my eyes open with his fingers.

"I can't look at them," I would cry. "Please don't make me."

But he would scream back, "Look! See what I went through! Look!"

Even though my work in the sex industry was the source of so much of Keith's anger, he still didn't have a job to support us. I couldn't read or write well enough to get by at what the Vagrants would call a citizen's job, so—having no education, skill, or self-confidence—I went back to the only thing I knew how to do: dance and hustle drinks. I had finally turned twenty and a day, so I could leave the peep shows for good and go back to the strip clubs.

I got in touch with one of my old managers, and he hired me on at his new club, the Sunset Lounge. It was a small hole-in-the-wall located in the center of downtown Louisville. Some people assume that being a dancer is a glamorous job and that it is like going to a party every night. However, there is nothing glamorous about having your backside patted all the time or old men trying to kiss you. And although I had always loved music, it was the last thing I wanted to hear after a long night of it blaring at the bar, and unlike many women my age, I had no interest in going to another bar or nightclub to enjoy a night with friends after work.

Although the Sunset Lounge might have felt like a party to the customers who walked in, to us dancers, it was a finely tuned operation. If it wasn't your turn to dance, you were expected to work the room nonstop, floating around entertaining the crowd until you found someone to spend money on you—in other words, buy you drinks for which both you and the bar got a cut of the money.

Then you found a corner table and flirted with the customer to make him think he was going to receive something in return for buying you drinks—all the while pushing his hands away to keep him from fondling and kissing you. You continued to drink each cocktail as quickly as possible and hoped that he liked you well enough to keep buying them every ten minutes so the manager wouldn't get angry with you for spending so much time with one man.

Most bars made you pay a fee to work there, and you had to earn more than the amount of the fee before you actually got to take home any money. You earned money primarily by selling drinks, of which the bar gave you maybe fifty percent of the profits. So if a bar charged you a hundred dollars to work for a night, you had to sell two hundred dollars' worth of drinks before you saw the first red cent from your labor. Some nights you might not make any money at all or might even owe the house money.

And then of course, there were the fines. If you violated any of the club's rules, they would dock your earnings different amounts depending on the severity of your action. For example, you could get fined for not being dressed and on the floor on time, not being onstage on time for your set, staying on a drink too long before convincing the customer to buy another, and leaving your shift early. The rules around fines constantly changed and were different with every club. And the clubs had different ways of keeping track of how many drinks you sold— whether tickets, receipts, or chips. At the end of the night, you received whatever you earned (minus the work fee and any fines), and you just had to hope that you weren't so drunk that someone stole your tickets or the bartender shorted you.

Drink quotas were a constant topic of conversation in the dressing room as girls worried about whether they would go home with any money. In those days, dancers weren't allowed to accept tips, so for many of us, meeting our drink quota meant the difference between being able to pay rent or not. I made very little money at the Sunset Lounge because business was usually slow. The real cash cow was the club across the street, where the girls danced nude and the money they made was insane.

But I made enough to keep Keith and me afloat, at least until I discovered I was pregnant again. Like before, I danced until it was obvious that I was pregnant. When that time arrived, the owner gave me a job behind the bar, where I made twenty dollars a night plus tips and whatever drinks I could sell.

Bartending was a highly coveted position because it was guaranteed pay plus the possibility of tips. I was surprised that I was capable of being trained for the job at all, much less able do it for four or five months. However, because I lacked any math skills, someone else always had to count my drawer for me at the end of my shift. I felt stupid standing by as others counted the money and filled out the report each morning when we closed. If the drawer was ever short what was supposed to be in it, I had to pay the bar back with my own money, which did happen occasionally. And without the ability to double-check others' work, I never knew if I was being cheated or if the drawer was truly short.

As the pregnancy progressed, I wasn't aware that I was carrying twins, but my little body was as my feet would swell and my back would be in agony from standing for eight to nine hours a night behind the bar. I was conditioned to work in the industry no matter how I felt or how little I wanted to, and this was no different.

Whenever customers came up to the bar to order a drink, I would hide my belly under the bar and rest my swollen breasts on top of it as I reached into the cooler for a beer or poured liquor from the well. I continued to hustle drinks just as I had as a dancer, except now I drank juice or Kool-Aid while pretending to the customer that it was a mixed drink. Only when I had to come out from behind the bar did a customer know I was pregnant.

"Hey, you're pregnant! You didn't tell me you were pregnant!" they would say.

I would laugh and reply, "You didn't ask."

I tried to make a joke out of it, and usually they tipped me well because I looked so desperate.

I worked up until the day before I was induced into labor. I was so happy to have a break from work that I felt like I was going on vacation. But before I left, the other dancers surprised me by throwing the biggest baby shower ever right there in the bar. Their gifts and generosity were an even greater blessing when I came home from the hospital with two babies instead of one—something for which Keith and I never could have prepared.

In contrast to the support I received at work, Keith continued his hatefulness and abuse throughout my pregnancy. We still lived with his parents, which was not a healthy environment, but it felt like we had no other choice since Keith still couldn't find a job. And although Keith was determined that his children would not carry Dirty Dan's last name, I was the one who had to drag him out from under a car that he was working on to go to the courthouse and get married late into my pregnancy. I didn't want what happened to me after Sara was born to happen again, so I married him hoping we could forget all that had happened with our first baby.

So I worked my last day behind the bar, and the following day, I was placed in the hospital and my labor was induced. Labor was so different this time; instead of a spirit of death hanging around me, there was the promise of life—and more life than I could have imagined, because I hadn't known all these months that I was carrying twins.

After the darkness of abortion and stillbirth, I finally gave birth to my first living baby, Terry. He was a little guy, weighing only four pounds and three ounces. But he was perfect to me, and even in my post-labor exhaustion, my heart was so full finally holding one of my babies in my arms.

Mary Lynn made her way into the world soon after, but immediately after she was born, the room was quiet; I heard no cry. Mere hours ago, I hadn't known this baby existed, but already I couldn't imagine life without her. Memories of Sara's birth now came crashing down on me, and I thought I too might stop breathing.

The doctor and nurses left me and ran to my baby. My whole body was shaking, and I gripped the sides of the bed so hard my knuckles turned white. Then finally, I heard her cry, and I collapsed back, thinking, *Thank God! Thank God my baby is alive.*

Once the baby was breathing, the doctor came back to me with a concerned look on his face. He told me not to be shocked when I saw my baby, because she too was small (less than four pounds) and she had been born with a cleft lip and palate. He said she would need a great deal of care and may not make it past her second birthday. But I didn't care what she looked like as I took her in my arms and promised her, "I'll do everything I can to fix you, baby. Just let Mama get some rest and I'll take care of you."

Since the twins were born premature, they didn't come home with me when I was released from the hospital. So once again I left the hospital without a baby, but every day I went to the nursery to check on my sweet babies. Someone made the remark that God had given me two babies in place of Sara. But as much as I loved my twins, I knew nothing could replace her.

Terry came home first, but Mary Lynn had to stay behind in the hospital because she had a sodium deficiency. Once she was released, the hospital didn't give me any instructions on how to feed her; they just gave me some tubes and plastic syringes and sent me home. She had a natural need to suck, but since she had no upper lip or palate, she would choke on the formula. I would hold her straight up or sit her in a carrier to feed her by placing this tube in her mouth while I pushed the formula out through the tube.

She would try and suck, and I would do everything trying to get the formula in her. She would cry, and then I would cry. I finally cut big holes in the nipples of her bottles and put the nipple on the side of her mouth that contained some palate, and she learned to bite down, causing the milk to come out very fast and often take her breath away. But between Mary Lynn and me, we figured it out through many tears.

By the time the twins were several months old, I finally convinced Keith to rent a small three-room house down the street from his parents. Our new family of four had been living cramped in his parents' storage room, with the twins sleeping in a single crib and waking each other up constantly. I wanted us to be our own family, and now that I was back to work, we could afford it, even though Keith continued to hate how I supported us.

Even when the twins got their own cribs, I got less and less sleep as they got older, especially with my work schedule at the clubs. Although Mary Lynn was a quiet and content baby, Terry was fussy and wanted to be held all the time. I had never liked children before I had my own, and it was difficult to adjust to caring for two all of a sudden. When we were young, my girlfriends would play with babies and gush over them, but I was usually annoyed and wanted nothing to do with them. But I tried very hard to connect with my twins; I wanted to bond with them, but lack of sleep and drama with their father was wearing me thin, leaving me with less patience. Often I would scream, "Shut up!" at them and then feel guilty for it.

The guilt of not knowing what to do and questioning everything I did haunted me. I wanted the best for my children and hated myself for not feeling warm and fuzzy inside toward them. I sensed something wasn't right and wanted to do something about it, but I had no one to turn to and no example to follow. I obsessed over their every need to the point of exhaustion and then went to work all night six days a week. All the while, the doctor's warning that Mary Lynn would die before she reached two years old hung over my head as I waited for death to claim yet another one of my children.

Still, I wasn't willing to let Mary Lynn go down without a fight. The first thing I did each morning when I came home from work was to run into the bedroom to cuddle, change, and feed the babies before getting them ready for early-morning doctor appointments. Mary Lynn had a whole team of specialists we had to go to every week to repair her face and see to her other health problems. Plastic surgeons; chromosome doctors; nutritionists; ear, nose, and throat doctors; sodium doctors; eye specialists for when she had symptoms of glaucoma; and doctors who put in palate implants to help her eat—that was how we spent our days. Then there were baby shots, colds, and illnesses, and well checkups with the pediatricians and clinics. The clinics lasted all day, and I rarely had anyone to help me. And if that wasn't enough, there were also WIC appointments so I could get free formula and juice for them.

Appointments and then more appointments, home for a quick nap and to satisfy their father, then make supper and run back to the bar to dance all night. I was so tired, and it never stopped. I wasn't even aware at first that Keith was having another affair—this time with a dancer. After all the years of harassment and abuse over me working in the industry, here he was leaving his children with his mother when I thought he was watching them so he could cheat on me with a dancer.

Eventually, he stopped trying to hide the affair and would disappear for long stretches of time. I started missing work because I didn't have anyone to watch the twins. Sometimes he came home long enough to wake me up, have his way with me, and then leave without a word to go pick up this other woman. I was so afraid of him that all I could do was lie there and cry once he had gone. I guess I felt my entertaining men for money gave him the right to treat me as he did, and yet he had chosen another dancer just to hurt me. At any time, I would have gladly hung up my dancing shoes and stayed home to care for my babies. But I felt I had no choice; I had to do the only thing I felt I was competent to do.

The breaking point came when Mary Lynn was in the hospital for one of her surgeries. As with most of her medical care, Keith was nowhere to be found, leaving me alone to care for Terry while staying with Mary Lynn at the hospital. Eventually, he showed up with his new girlfriend tagging along. The feeling was oh so familiar. Here I was in the hospital with one of our children when I needed him most, and he showed up late with another woman hanging on his arm.

He didn't ask about Mary Lynn; it was clear he had come just to shove this girl in my face. I watched this woman I didn't know pick up my child while Keith—the one who was supposed to protect and provide for us—told me I would just have to "get used to it."

I was so angry, partly because I was grieving yet another rejection from him but mostly because he was using my child's health as an occasion to bring around this strange woman. If I hadn't thought I would go to jail and put my child in jeopardy, I would have done something crazy right there in the hospital room. I wanted to wipe the floor with this woman and then kick them both out of the hospital myself. But I knew if I didn't restrain myself, they or the hospital staff would call the police, and I might lose my babies forever. So I had to say nothing and sit back and watch all of this unfold. After they left, I waited for my baby to fall asleep, and then I sat next to the window looking out at the city and cried.

Once we got home from Mary Lynn's surgery and she was healed, Keith returned and claimed he wanted to come back to us. But I could never forgive him for bringing his girlfriend to the hospital while our daughter was having surgery, and I told him so—loudly. He yelled and flung all the familiar abuses, but I wasn't having it this time.

Finally, he grabbed both babies, and carrying one under each arm like footballs, he stormed out the door. They were both screaming and crying, and I had never felt so helpless and defenseless as he carried my babies away from me. I knew he was taking them to his parents' house to hold them hostage until I came back to him. But I didn't know what violence awaited me if I went back to him yet again, and I could never forget the sight of another woman holding my child.

For months, I had had the number of a battered women's shelter but had never had the courage to go there. As much as Keith had abused me, I had never been so scared as when he took my babies. Not knowing what to do and with nowhere else to turn, I called and then checked myself into the shelter. I met with a crisis counselor, who took notes as I shared my stories of abuse. I was issued a room and was given something to eat by one of the residents.

Once alone in my room, I lay on the bed and whimpered and wept for my babies. Mary Lynn had appointments this week, and I wondered if he would keep them. Were they hungry? Would Keith know how to feed Mary Lynn? Would Terry ever settle down if I wasn't there to hold him? Would Keith make sure they didn't get a diaper rash? Would they even fit in that one crib in the storage room anymore? My mind raced as I tossed and turned all night, wondering when I would see my babies again.

# CHAPTER FIFTEEN

# Retired Hooker

I had made it to the women's shelter and finally was free from Keith. It was the first battered women's shelter in Louisville that I knew of, maybe the first in Kentucky. It was in the YMCA, and we had to be locked in for our protection. To my dismay, I had to deal with Child Protective Services and the court system to divorce Keith. But I had to get my babies back. God help me, he had finally done what he threatened all along to do if I should leave him, but I was going to make it right.

I told myself I would no longer work in the bars. Keith would try to use my past against me to keep my babies from me, but I wasn't going to let him. The first step was to gather my courage and go to court to file an emergency protective order.

Even though I was there to get help, my stomach was in knots as I explained to the clerk, "He walked out with the babies and refuses to give them back. He's acting like a biker."

At that, the clerk slammed down the notepad she had been writing on, nearly making me jump. "I've had enough of bikers beating up on their women this week," she said.

Then she took me into the judge's chambers. After hearing

my testimony, the judge placed an order for the sheriffs to go get my babies and bring them to the shelter with me.

Once back at the shelter, I waited anxiously in the hall downstairs for the police and social workers to show up with the twins. I finally saw them through the windows, and they looked confused and frightened until they saw me. Once they were in my arms, I kissed their faces and hugged them and promised I was going to do whatever it took to take care of us. I knew that meant working somewhere other than the bars because I knew Keith was going to use it against me in court.

The twins and I settled into the shelter together, and even though I was frightened by the prospect of all the court dates and changes that were coming, I knew we were in the right place. For the first time in my life, I got to talk with a counselor and go to group therapy where other women had something in common with me: pain. We learned how to vent without hurting others, and we talked about the importance of boundaries. I had no idea what a boundary was, but I was told I didn't have any. The shelter taught me how to look for and apply for a citizen's job, and for the first time ever, I thought I might be able to do something outside the sex industry.

All the while, I would look out the window and see Keith's car in the parking lot. The shelter kept him locked out, and I couldn't leave the building either while I waited for our court date for a divorce. Some of the other women would leave the shelter and go back to their abusive partners, but I stayed strong and stayed put.

While I waited for the court date, I began to look for work, filling out application after application. My journey for work took me to a restaurant and night club called the Riverside Saloon. I applied for a server and cocktail waitress position, and not long after the interview, I received the call that I got the job. I was nervous and overwhelmed but still determined to do what I had to for my children.

The court date for the divorce came, and I settled for twenty-five dollars a week in child support for both children as long as I could have custody.

After six months in the shelter, I finally felt safe enough to move into an apartment in the poorest area of the city. I continued to attend my support group at the shelter and stayed in touch with many of the former residents. Now in my early twenties, I was trying desperately to build the support system that I had never had before; however, I was running out of babysitters to help while I worked.

Although they never visited or offered any help, I did long to live closer to my parents, who were now remarried to each other and living in another part of town. In the past few years while my life had been in chaos, both my stepmother and stepfather, Tucker, had died, and my parents had found their way back to each other after all those years apart.

My stepmother had finally lost her battle against her illness, and Tucker passed away after a bad lung infection and other complications. I believe I was the last person to see him alive when I visited him on Father's Day. When I entered the hospital room, he asked the orderly to cover him up because his daughter was here. It was the first time in my life he had called me his daughter, and I was shocked and touched. I wished him a happy Father's Day, not knowing that would be the last time I would see him.

Tucker had always been a stable figure in my childhood, and I wished he could have been the same for my children as their lives started to look more and more like mine had been when I was their age. The apartment that we were living in reminded me of the apartment I was abandoned in as a child.

The same staircase. The same tall ceilings. The same roaches. The freezing cold in the winter and blistering hot in the summer.

But the rent was only a hundred and fifty dollars a month with utilities included, and my sister-in-law and niece lived below me and my cousin Dolores lived in the alley behind me with her two boys. I tried very hard to keep the apartment clean, but whenever I turned on the lights in the kitchen, I would be met with the sight of roaches covering the ceiling and walls.

My niece moved in with me for a while to help with the twins, but I always gave her a hard time. I would say things like, "You can't leave even one dish in the sink. CPS will take my babies, so the apartment has to be clean all the time. They can't have a diaper rash or I'll lose them."

After the incident with Keith and having to go through the court to get them back, I had so much unnecessary anxiety about losing my children. My social worker told me I was a good mother, but nothing could convince me she was telling the truth. I called CPS all the time to check in because I thought that if they were already in my life, then I wouldn't have to worry about someone else calling them on me.

I had a sick way of trying to control situations because of my fear. I had stayed with two men who abused me because I was more afraid of them being out of sight and potentially coming after me like the demons in my dreams. My controlling nature finally drove my niece away, and she moved back downstairs with her mother.

I thought I was staying a step ahead of the world, but in reality, I was floundering. I had to find another babysitter so I could work, but it was so hard to find someone I could trust. Finally, I discovered that one of the girls I had met in the battered women's shelter lived only blocks away from my apartment. We had been in the same support group, and she had two young daughters for my children to play with. I was so relieved when she agreed to watch the twins.

I had one umbrella stroller that I would strap both twins into to take them to their babysitter before I caught the bus to work. Because she was smaller, Mary Lynn would sit on Terry's lap, and he would hold on to his sister to protect her from falling out. Although it seemed like the perfect solution at first, I started to feel uneasy about leaving them with my friend from the shelter. There were always several young men hanging around the front yard, and she would sit on the porch steps talking to them at all hours of the day and night. Even the twins started to cry and not want to stay when I tried to drop them off.

One night when I had to go to work, Terry had a fever and sore throat. I packed their bags with medicine, pajamas, and soda for him. The stroller was broken, so I had my nephew help me carry the twins and their things to my friend's apartment. She was waiting for us on the steps, and Terry started crying, not wanting to stay.

I told her Terry was sick and instructed her on when and how to give him the medicines I had in the bag. She assured me that she would take care of them. I kissed and hugged my babies as the guilt of leaving them behind flooded my body. My nephew and I then left and began to walk back to the apartment so I could catch the bus.

As we turned the corner, I couldn't bear it any longer. I looked at my nephew and said, "I can't do this. I can't leave my sick baby. He needs me."

I went back around the corner, my nephew right behind me, just in time to witness this woman yanking my sick child by the arm and shouting, "Get your a—— in the house!"

I was shocked. No wonder my children cried when I left them here. I felt a surge of electricity run up my spine, and I started running toward her screaming, "Take your damn hands off my child!"

The woman let go immediately, and Terry rushed into my arms. "Where is my daughter?" I snapped at the woman. "Mary Lynn!"

Mary Lynn came running out of the house with a smile on her face, and I took her hand too. "Come on, we're going home. Mama's not working tonight."

I should have beaten that woman, but I wouldn't even let myself speak to her as I took my babies home. I spent the evening comforting and caring for my child myself, and the next day when she called me, I told her she would not be paid for mistreating my babies. Worried for my babies' welfare, I went through sitter after sitter until I finally reconnected with another woman from the shelter whom I always called Nana.

Unlike the woman who had been cruel to my children, Nana cared for them as if they were her own, and she came to care for me like a mother too. She took the children at all hours of the day and night, even when I had to work until five in the morning. We were taking the twins back and forth between our homes so often that I sometimes stayed at her house just to get the extra sleep. She even let me stay there alone when she took the twins to church on Sunday morning.

I was still having terrible nightmares about demons and bikers, and I often woke from a deep sleep screaming and running down the hall. Nana would chase me down during these fits, wake me up, and tell me, "Give it to Jesus, Mary, and peace will come over you. He is the only hope we have." When she spoke about God, it reminded me of the people who protested outside the peep shows and strip clubs, and the shame and guilt I felt when I passed them on my way to work. But at least I knew Nana meant well, even if I didn't think much of her advice.

Things started looking up too when my aunt offered to rent me her old house in Butchertown. Although it was roach-free and closer to work, it still had its own haunting reminders of my past, as it sat across the street from an old whorehouse that Dirty Dan had placed me in before the Paradise Garden Massage Parlor. The building was a furniture repair shop now, but I still remembered being sixteen years old and sneaking in and out of the place, hoping my aunt wouldn't see me from across the street and know that I was working as a prostitute. Now every time I stepped out of my new house, the memories flooded my mind of a time and place that was hidden in the darkest parts of my heart. Although I was trying to make a better life for myself and my children, it seemed as if there was no getting away from my past, no matter how hard I tried.

The bright spot of being back in Butchertown was that I was again close to the Wesley House Community Center, where I had spent the precious few hours of happiness in my childhood. Now my children attended there as well, and they were never the last to be picked up.

Although I was so thankful to have a clean home and a real friend in Nana, my heart was still lonely for romance. I had never been on a real date—one where a man picked you up, took you to dinner, and paid for the meal and a movie. Coffee with a boy from the picture booths hardly seemed to count now that I was in my twenties. All the other servers at work were dating busboys or bartenders, and everyone else seemed to have dates for our company parties while I showed up alone. Nana tried to comfort me by telling me that I didn't need a man; all I needed was Jesus. It took a lifetime to realize how right she was, but my need for love ruled over the empty spot in my soul.

Unfortunately, lack of a boyfriend was the least of my troubles at work. I worried constantly about being discovered for the fraud I felt I was. Even after working there for two years, I couldn't comprehend the wine list or menu. I had never eaten things like fettuccine Alfredo (and didn't really know what it was either), and I could never organize myself enough to handle large dinner parties.

My boss started assigning me shifts known not to make any money, and if a headliner was in the saloon, I was given the area outside the saloon, where there would be no tips all evening. Sometimes I took on minimum-wage tasks such as dishwashing and food prep; I was even a clown once at one of our events. And all the while, I was convinced that if they found out who I really was and what I had been, I would be fired and my time among citizens would come to an end.

My worst fears came true when one day as I was cleaning off tables in my station, a coworker said to me in front of everyone, "Mary, aren't you a retired hooker?"

The customers and other waitstaff overheard what he said, and it felt like every head in the place snapped in my direction. Mortified, I tried to play it off like I hadn't heard him, but I could feel all eyes on me as everyone stopped talking.

I continued to wipe down tables, trying to get as far away from him as possible, all the while remembering what dirt I was. I made it to the breakroom, but it was full of people. I tried fleeing to the locker room, but there were people there too. Finally, I went into the employee bathroom to hang my head and cry. The shame, emptiness, and loneliness of the past months was setting in.

*Get up and get yourself together*, I told myself. *It's almost closing time, and you have to suck it up.* I asked one of the girls who was always kind to me to help me clock out because I always slowed everyone down at the terminal, and then I left the second my shift was over.

I took a cab home, got my babies from my cousin Dolores, and cried myself to sleep. The next day, I confronted the general manager about the insult. I lied and said I wasn't an ex-prostitute even though I knew he must have known the truth about me. You can't hide something like that; it shows in the way people look at you, and it made me want to go back to where I felt I belonged. And where I belonged certainly was not in this fine establishment with intelligent people who had nice things and educations and vocabularies that I couldn't keep up with.

If that incident wasn't enough to bring me down, my mother would top it later that week when she showed up to Riverside drunk. It was a beautiful day, and I was working on the rooftop garden, where plants hung throughout the bar like a jungle. My feet were aching because we were required to wear pumps, and the floor of the garden was made up of pea gravel, which made it difficult to carry heavy trays in heels.

I was waiting my turn at the register to put in an order when I overheard one waitress tell another that there were three nasty women in a booth and one had pulled out a liquor bottle to pour whiskey into her Coke. I laughed with them and placed my order.

But when I walked past the table with the three women, I saw that it was my mother and two of my aunts. My mother was drunk and sitting there with a beer between her legs. One aunt was as drunk as my mother, and the other was sober. They had all been to the racetrack that day and decided to come see me.

When my mother caught sight of me, she yelled, "Hey, Mary, bring your a—— over here! I wanted to show your aunts where you work now."

Like when the other waiter had called me a retired hooker, everyone looked around at me. I wanted to run and hide, but I knew if I ignored my mother, she would make an even bigger scene. So, my cheeks burning, I walked over to their table.

My mother looked like she hadn't showered in days. She wore flip-flops that revealed her dirty ingrown toenails, and her shirt was filthy and tight across her belly. Her hair was a mess, and it smelled as if she had urinated on herself. She could not have been more out of place among Riverside's business and upper-class clientele.

"What are you doing here, Mama? I'm trying to work," I whispered. I turned to my aunt. "Please put that bottle away. It's illegal to bring in your own liquor, and you're pouring it into your soda right here in front of everybody. Please put it away."

"I just wanted to show everybody where you worked, Mary," Mama said. She too had lowered her voice.

"Okay, Mama. I've got to go back to work. I'll see you later."

I think my mother really was proud of me and wanted to show her sisters that I had changed. But that didn't help the humiliation I felt in that moment. I made my way back to the waitress station, where all I found waiting for me was a sick silence. I hung my head in shame. No one said anything, but they all knew that the woman in the booth was my mother. They must have felt sorry for me and were embarrassed for me as well.

That night when I got home, I was exhausted and drained of every emotion but shame. Both incidents happened in the same week, and I was convinced that I had to get back to where I fit in, where I was the best. Where there was no emotion, no judgment. Where I could make money and not be reminded of my past, but instead live the life that refused to stop following me no matter where I went. The place where I could be the classiest and the best at the job I knew. Where I was respected and cared about by the women I worked with and where I made enough money to live. And more importantly, when my babies needed me, especially Mary Lynn, I could take off without being fired or harassed about what I needed to do for her.

The temptation to return to the sex industry haunted me for days. In one last-ditch effort, I sought out another cocktail waitress job at a different restaurant in hopes that I might be able to start over at someplace other than the Riverside Saloon. Nana loaded me and the kids in her Volkswagen Bug and drove me to the interview. When we arrived and I stepped out of the car, I saw all the pretty young women standing outside of the establishment waiting to apply for the same job.

Nana seemed to sense my sudden wave of doubt and said, "I know what you're thinking, Mary. You're just as good as they are. Don't let the devil tell you otherwise."

I got back in the car, my eyes stinging with tears. "I can't do this, Nana," I said. "This is just like Riverside. I'm too low class for a place like this."

The year was 1986, and I was twenty-six years old. My emotions were stunted from suppressing them all these years. I questioned everything about myself and was frightened of everything outside my comfort zone—however awful that comfort zone was. Within the deepest parts of my soul were dirty secrets and a lack of education and lack of God. How could I work in nice, classy places when what was inside me was anything but?

Nana told me I just needed to build confidence to work with the public, and I knew she was right. But she and I also knew that I would choose the strip club over any place where I felt insecure. It was exhausting to work at a place where I had to pretend I could read and act like I hadn't come from white trash. I told myself it was the money in the strip club that I was returning to, but it wasn't. It was the one place in the world where my shame was safe.

# CHAPTER SIXTEEN

# Sugar and Spice

Not long after I had decided I couldn't make it any longer at Riverside, I ran across my old manager from the Sunset Lounge. He told me about a place called Sugar and Spice and the money everyone was making there. Unlike any other bar in town, Sugar and Spice allowed the dancers to take tips onstage, which was a sure way to make money faster than only hustling drinks. Sugar and Spice was close to Nana's apartment too, and after the humiliation I had suffered among my coworkers at Riverside, I didn't need much more incentive to go back to what I knew best.

When you entered Sugar and Spice, it took a few moments for your eyes to adjust to the dark. The brightest light inside shone over the cash register behind the bar, while the stage had multiple blue and red spotlights and a mirrored ball hanging over it. Immediately you could smell sour bourbon and see cigarette smoke, as it hung heavy in the spotlights pointing at the stage.

In those days, the club had two different stages in two different rooms, separated by a hallway. On one side of the club, girls danced topless and alcohol was served, but on the other side, girls danced completely nude. All of the dancers worked both sides depending on crowd size. However, what went on on the nude side was completely out of my league. Some girls would do just about anything for a dollar, and their routines were so provocative that they were hard to follow. So I stuck with what I was used to—hustling drinks and receiving a few tips here and there.

No matter the season, I always felt cold in Sugar and Spice from drinking iced-down cocktails and wearing very little clothing. However, before I could go onstage and let my dance routine warm me up, I had to collect money to play my songs on the jukebox. Every girl would walk among the crowd and ask the men, "Got a dollar for the jukebox?"

Once we got three dollars, that was enough for a three-song set, which we got to pick out ourselves. In the old days, the jukebox had vinyl forty-five records that each had only one song, so the same few numbers would play over and over all year long. But now we had CDs with entire albums to choose from. All the girls would try to find the longest songs in the jukebox to ensure more time for tips onstage.

While the customers watched us, we dancers watched ourselves in the mirrors along the back wall of the stage. The bar where the liquor was served wasn't much of a bar, as it contained only two barstools and a waitress station. Instead, the stage acted as the bar, wrapping completely around the room on the lower level. A few partitioned tables were reserved for those of us who sold cocktails or bottles of champagne.

The dressing room was just a step or two from the stage. Unlike the bar, this room was brightly lit so the girls could see every detail of themselves in the full-length mirrors nailed sideways along the wall. Ten worn-out chairs faced the home-made dressing table that had been braced to the wall. The table itself was just a few pieces of unpainted lumber littered with cigarette burns, dirt, makeup, and ashes. The floor was uneven and old, and the tile was worn out where each chair sat. Small broken gym lockers took up space in the corner, but the girls outnumbered the lockers, so they usually ended up throwing their dance bags under their feet as they got ready. The scent of Aqua Net hairspray and numerous perfumes and body sprays often took my breath away. At any time, ten or more naked women would cram themselves in front of mirrors to apply thick layers of makeup and do their hair before going out on the floor.

My routine included curling my hair, applying makeup, putting on my costume, and dabbing on a musk perfume called Skin. Then I took two Tylenol (in anticipation of the back ache that always showed up during the night) and two allergy pills to keep my nose from running due to the cigarette smoke that climbed to the top of the ceiling. I never wanted the customers to see me wipe my nose like the other girls did; I thought that was so unattractive. Also unlike the other girls, who smuggled in bottles of liquor in their bags, I didn't do drugs or drink much before my shift. Rather, I drank a thermos of coffee throughout the night to stay awake after being up all day for the twins' doctor appointments.

My one exception to not drinking was to take a shot of bourbon just before I went out to the floor to start my hustle. Then, once out of the dressing room, I would look out over the crowd to read the men and make my mark. Somehow I always knew who to hustle; I could read the loneliness that was obvious through their body language.

However, in a world where there were no boundaries, I had established at least one personal rule about hustling: I would not take money from a man who I knew had a family at home. In fact, I would tell him to take his money home to pay his rent and hope that one of the many other sharks (that is, dancers) wouldn't get to him before he left. I couldn't bring myself to rob a child's father if I knew it was payday and he had just stopped in for a beer. I would discourage him from blowing his money even though most of the girls would sit there until his last red cent was gone. But I couldn't lower myself to the level of the cutthroats, because I could never forget my mother's stories about my father spending all his money on prostitutes rather than his family.

Later in life, I would expand my rule to include men who were close to my sons' ages. But for now, I was young and unhindered, and so once I found a suitable target, I unleashed all my charms on him. For example, one night, I noticed a man who was so short and compact that I knew he had to be a horse jockey. Since Churchill Downs was just a few miles away, this was not an unheard-of occurrence. Being petite myself, I knew we had something in common, and that was all I needed to make my move. I sat down at his table and made burning eye contact with him while I smiled and brushed my leg against his.

"What's your name?" I asked, carefully timing myself so as not to appear too hungry.

After he told me, I continued, "Would you care to buy me something to drink and share what's on your mind?"

"Sure," he replied. "What would you like?"

"Hmm, what would I like?" I ran my fingers through my hair, trying to appear innocent. "Well, when I want to feel really good, I drink champagne."

"Then champagne it is," he declared.

"It's really expensive though," I replied, trying to sound concerned. "It costs a hundred dollars a bottle."

All the clubs sold the cheapest champagne on the market

and marked it up a ridiculous amount, and the hangover from it was so bad that it often kept you from working the next day. The waitress brought us our first bottle, and I sipped on a glass of the nastiest drink I had ever consumed until it was my turn to dance. Then, while I was onstage, my jockey tipped me with a hundred dollar bill. When I was finished with my set, I went back to his table to work through the first bottle. And then another and another until he had paid for at least a dozen bottles of champagne.

The hustle was on, and all the other girls hated me as they watched me work. Each time I danced, he slipped me another hundred dollar bill, and then I pretended to enjoy the champagne. I sipped only a small amount of each glass and poured the rest into the ice bucket on the floor whenever I returned the champagne bottle to it. The bucket was soon full of the champagne, even though I often missed the bucket and instead poured my drink onto the floor.

After a while of doing this, my jockey leaned into me and said, "I'll buy you anything you want if you just stop pouring champagne in my shoes."

We both laughed. He didn't mind; he just wanted someone to talk to and hug on—someone who would pretend to be his date for the night. When closing time came around, I had made more than seventeen hundred dollars. The next day, even though I had drunk very little, I nursed a champagne hangover and took two days off to recover. But on the second day, I bought new clothes, toys, and goodies for my babies and paid all the bills for the month.

The night with the jockey was like hitting the strip-club jackpot. But for every night like that, there was a week or more of dry spells and coming home without a dime. The real way to make money was to have regulars—men who came in to see you specifically and who were guaranteed to spend money on you in exchange for your attention and affection.

Early on in my career, the old manager of the Baby Dolls strip club had told me that it took only one customer. And he was right. If one man came in once or twice a week and spent a hundred dollars on you, that was as close to steady income as you could get in my world. And if you had more than one man doing that, then you were really in business. Men like that represented your bills getting paid and your children getting clothed. And that was precisely the kind of man Eric was.

I had worked at Sugar and Spice for a week or so when Eric approached me to say I had beautiful eyes. Then he began trying to impress me by buying twenty-dollar drinks as fast as I could drink them. After a hundred dollars of gin and tonic with a twist of lime, I told the waitress in secret, "Make it just tonic water and hold the gin."

Eric bought me one after the other until he had spent close to two hundred dollars. Unlike with the jockey, when my mind had been completely occupied with how to trick him out of more money, I found myself really enjoying Eric's conversation and his attention toward me. Dirty Dan had always warned me not to become personally involved with customers, but after being alone for so long since Keith, Eric was one of the first men who caught my eye and who I thought might actually be interested in me. When our hour and a half was over, I had not only a wad of cash, but also his phone number.

Once Eric was gone, I couldn't get him off my mind. I called him often in the coming weeks, and although he didn't call me as much as I called him, I was always thrilled when I saw him walk through the door of Sugar and Spice. Once I got off the stage, we would find a table and he would buy me ten-dollar drinks instead of the twenty-dollar ones he had bought the night I met him.

The dancers weren't allowed to entertain or have conversations with a man for very long without a cocktail in hand, and Eric knew this; so he bought me the cheapest drink you could hustle, and I nursed it as long as I could just so I could spend time with him. The waitress kept coming back to our table and asking, with a pointed look, if I needed another drink. It was part of a waitress's job to hustle the customer along with the dancers and to make sure the dancers didn't sit on a drink too long or pocket money that belonged to the bar.

One night, Eric and I decided to finally meet up outside of work. He stopped by Nana's house that day before I left for work, and Nana was not impressed. "That man is very arrogant," she told me after he left. "You shouldn't be looking for a man; you should be looking for Jesus."

As with most of her advice, I shrugged it off and went to work. Later that night, I called Eric from the bar phone and made plans for him to pick me up and take me to a party he was throwing at his house. So at two in the morning, I paid out my quota of two twenty-dollar drinks plus two additional ones for leaving early, and then hopped into Eric's car.

Eric's house impressed me even more than he had that first night when he had bought me all those twenty-dollar drinks. When I had worked at the Sunset Lounge, I would drive past the grand old houses like his in Old Louisville and wonder what was inside. Now was finally my chance to see. His house was spotless, and fancy decorations hung on the walls and fancy knickknacks sat on the fancy tables. Even the white carpet in his living room was free of any stains; I had never even seen white carpet before, much less seen something like that kept so clean. I suddenly felt ashamed of myself; here I was, a child of the projects, coming into such a fine house.

Perhaps Eric was out of my league after all.

We stood at his bar, and I gazed at the bottles of his expensive champagne. The difference between these bottles and the bottles they sold at Sugar and Spice was that these really did cost a hundred dollars at the liquor store. Later, Eric grilled out steaks, and I was so impressed with his cooking; I never ate or drank anything like this. But he didn't know that, and I didn't care to reveal myself for the imposter I was—at least not yet.

From that night on, I was completely hooked. I saw Eric whenever I could—or, more accurately, whenever he would have me. Nana did not stand for men staying at her house, so I paid her to sit for the twins not only while I was at work, but also when I went out with Eric. It wasn't long before I loved every fiber in his being, simply because he showed me very little attention.

Sometimes he would avoid my calls for days or promise to meet me and then never show up. But by the time he came back around, I was so lonely that it was easy for him to take advantage of my weakness. Nana kept insisting that a man would never fill the void I was feeling, but nothing could stop me from trying to fill it anyway. I knew something had always been missing in my life, and I was searching like a mad woman for it.

As much as I would have liked to hide it after seeing Eric's house, it didn't take long for him to come to the house that I rented from my aunt. To say the least, my house was not as fancy as his, and I was so embarrassed because the house had roaches that I had carried with us from the first apartment that I had rented after leaving the shelter. Eric was finding out who I really was—including the fact that I had once been a biker's ol' lady—and the more he learned, the less he saw of me. He only called me when he had nothing better to do, and I was convinced he didn't love me because I was uneducated and came from low-class people.

One day during one of our stretches of not seeing each other, I felt a sharp pain in my side. It was so bad that I called in to take the night off work even though my paycheck would be docked for doing so. For several days, I laid in bed in a fetal position, unable to move and trying in vain to fight a growing fever. I couldn't find Eric, so eventually I called Nana and asked her to take me to the emergency room. After examining me, the doctor diagnosed me with an atopic pregnancy and referred me back to my OB–GYN for surgery.

Ever since I had come so close to dying while giving birth to Sara, I had a deep-seated fear of dying in surgery. I fretted for days leading up to the surgery that would end this pregnancy, but when I finally found Eric to tell him what was going on, his only question was, "So we can get pregnant?"

"What do you mean by that?" I blurted.

"I want a son," he replied simply.

Although I dreaded the surgery and the loss of another pregnancy, those words gave me hope that Eric really did love me. After all, why else would he want me to have his son? Eric stayed with me in the hospital after surgery, but once I was home recovering, it was back to seeing him for a while and then him disappearing for weeks at a time.

The more he rejected me, the more I thought I loved him. I began to become depressed and thought I was going crazy, as all I could think about was Eric. Just when I thought I could forget him and move on, he would come back just long enough to start the cycle again. Finally, it got so unbearable that I reached out to my former child protection worker, who had opened her own counseling practice, and she agreed to help me walk through all of my emotional issues.

At one point, my therapist asked me what my goals and dreams were. No one had ever asked me a question like that. Life had always been about survival—nothing bigger or grander than that. But soon I confessed that I had always wanted to go back to school so I wouldn't feel so inferior like I had at the Riverside Saloon and around people like Eric. Like the houses in Old Louisville, I would always drive past the University of Louisville and wonder what it was like to be a student at such a prestigious place.

My therapist encouraged me to pursue my education; she said that having a goal to work toward would improve my mental and emotional state, not to mention open up new opportunities in life. There was a center not far from Sugar and Spice that would help me earn my GED, and once I had the idea in my head, I signed up immediately.

I started taking the bus from Nana's to the center to study for my GED and then later from the center to Sugar and Spice to work. Everywhere I went, I hauled around two bags: one with my study materials and another with my stage costumes. When business was slow, I studied in the dressing room and often got in trouble for being late for my set because I was trying to figure out simple division. But I didn't mind the new busyness of my life; I finally had something worth talking about at my therapy appointments, and my dream of going to U of L actually seemed in reach, even for a poor girl like me.

One day when I was waiting for the bus to take me from school to work, Eric pulled up along the curb and asked me if I wanted a ride to work. I hadn't seen him for some time, so my heart soared as I jumped into the van. We pulled into the parking lot of the club and talked for a while since I was early for work. He promised to pick me up and drive me home after work, and I spent the whole night giddy with anticipation.

But when four o'clock rolled around, he didn't show up. Disappointed, I took a cab home as usual. Several nights later, he called and acted as though I had no reason to be upset. It took him all of thirty minutes to convince me that I should let him come to the house. Little did I know how much letting my guard down like that would change my life.

For the next several weeks, it was back to therapy, school, and dancing. At therapy, it was talking and some new-age meditation, and at school, it was learning how to break down a fraction. Work was another world entirely; I continued to transform nightly into someone else so I could provide for my children. I was beginning to hate myself and thought often about my children and what they would think of me when they became old enough to understand what and who their mother really was. I had to get out, and I was convinced that education was my only way.

Finally, after almost a year of studying, I opened my mailbox to find a postcard that said, "Congratulations! You have received your GED." Instead of feeling excited, I was ashamed as I stood on my porch and read it. It wasn't good enough. A GED meant I never went to prom; it said something went wrong when I should have been in high school. I had gotten through the test, but I still couldn't read well enough to comprehend the daily newspaper.

Shortly after, I found out I was pregnant once again, and once again, Eric had disappeared. When I finally did catch up with him, I demanded, "Why do you always treat me this way? You come and go as you please, and you never think about what I need."

"I never said I wanted a relationship with you," he shot back. "I just want a son."

It was nothing I didn't already know deep down in my

heart, but hearing him say it out loud made me feel used like I had been so many times before. And as before with Sara and my twins, I continued to dance until I couldn't dance any longer. By the time I reached twenty-seven years old, I had worked in almost every club in the city—uptown and downtown as well as every club on the Seventh Street strip. And once my pregnancy started to show, there was no longer a job for me at Sugar and Spice, so it was back to the slums of the red light district to work as a bartender.

The bar was called Good Ol' Days and was located on Jefferson Street. To the right of Good Ol' Days was another bar where the local drunks hung out with the hookers and bums. To the left was the Fillies Theater, and on the corner was another peep show that I had worked in as a teenager. Prostitution was everywhere, and the bar owners had to chase them off occasionally so as not to get in trouble with the police. Homeless people wandered the streets, and you couldn't step in or out the door without being asked for change. In the wintertime, they squatted in the bars to stay warm.

Here I was working down in the pit of hell, GED and all. Meanwhile, my own parents were trying to edge me out of my aunt's house. Admittedly, I didn't want to stay there long anyway; the twins were nearing school age, and I didn't want them going to the same school I had after all the bad memories I had there. However, once my parents heard I wanted to move and decided they wanted to rent my aunt's house after me, they staked their claim by moving in with me before I moved out.

Thankfully, by the time I reached my ninth month of pregnancy, I had squirreled away a thousand dollars to get another place. However, two weeks before I gave birth, my manager told me he had to let me go because I was too big of a risk; he was afraid I would be hurt because of all of the unsavory people who hung around the bar. This left me jobless as I apartment-hunted. I had to convince landlords that once I had my baby, I would be able to pay rent; I just needed a place to stay for a month because my parents wanted me and the twins out of "their" house.

Just days before giving birth, I was saved the shame of being pregnant, jobless, and homeless when I found an apartment in a decent neighborhood. Nana moved into the same apartment building since it would be convenient for the both of us once I went back to work after the baby was born.

Just after we moved into the new place, I went into labor. When Eric couldn't get ahold of me at home, he knew where to find me—in the hospital, having his child. I hated to even let him in the room, so he stood outside and paced up and down the hall while I delivered the baby without the help of drugs for the pain. Once the baby arrived, I finally allowed Eric in to meet our seven-pound, eight-ounce baby boy named Ross, just as his father had ordered.

Eric was so proud as he held him in the sunlight coming through the window and checked out everything about him. As little as I wanted to see Eric, I also couldn't have been more proud of our baby, especially when the doctor told me that he was a 9.9 out of 10 on the Apgar scale. I promised myself that with Ross, I would be the perfect mother and learn to love and bond with him as I hadn't with my twins.

After the doctors telling me Mary Lynn would die before the age of two, I hadn't been able to bring myself to bond with one twin and not the other. It was always work, stress, and worry with my twins, but now I wanted very much to be a good mother to them all. So I told myself that with this baby, I would learn to be affectionate with my children and be the genuine mother I longed to be.

I took the next six weeks off work and did nothing but show Ross every ounce of attention I could find within myself. Meanwhile, the twins—now six years old—stood by waiting for this newfound love. Eric stayed with us for a short time, and then it was back to never hearing from him again. I would have loved to be a stay-at-home mom with them, but soon it was back to work at the bars while Nana cared for all three. Although I didn't know it, I would soon get my wish to be with my children full time, but I never could have imagined the price I would have to pay for it.

# CHAPTER SEVENTEEN

# Return to the Jungle

G ood Ol' Days had closed its doors, so once my maternity leave was over, I went back to Sugar and Spice. Business was still as good as before, if not better. The managers welcomed me back, and they understood that I had babies to care for and allowed me to take off whenever my responsibilities called me home. This was another reason to continue working in the clubs. No citizen's job would let me off work whenever I needed to take Mary Lynn to her multiple doctors and Ross to his newborn checkups and shot appointments.

I started to stay up all morning after work to make sure I didn't oversleep and miss getting Mary Lynn and Terry ready for school. If Mary Lynn had an appointment, that usually meant we had to spend all day at the clinic and would come home exhausted. It felt as if I hadn't slept in years, and in the daylight, away from the black lights of the club, anyone could see I was worn out.

Eric had informed me that he was seeing someone else, which confirmed that I was no more to him than an egg donor. Along with everything else, I continued to attend my therapy sessions, and all I talked about was how I wanted to be a good mother and go to college to be an example for my children.

My worst fears came true when Mary Lynn and Terry came home one day and showed me a project they had done in school. The assignment had been to look through magazines for pictures that reminded them of their mother and cut and paste them on a piece of paper. Terry had found pictures of a typical mother in a dress holding a tray of food. But Mary Lynn's project was a different story. She had cut out a picture of a woman who had spiked hair and wore a short skirt and stilettos. It shocked me to think my child perceived me in this way, but the image was accurate. She had seen me go to work dressed like this, and I couldn't help but feel that my daughter had joined the ranks of family and friends who were ashamed of me.

\*

"Mary, you're up," the manager hollered out to me.

I waded through the crowd and placed the three dollars I had just hustled into the jukebox to choose my three songs. Then I took to the stage to do what I had done since I was sixteen. Although I was short, my legs appeared long in my spike-heeled leather ankle boots. Where other girls would strip down to almost nothing, I never took off my French-cut leather jacket, leaving the mystery up to the psyche.

I strutted to the middle of the stage like I was worth a million bucks, ignoring the stripper poles because I had something original to offer. I gained speed and threw out both arms as I leaned my head on my shoulder, letting my hair fall over my face as I began to spin like Michael Jackson. I didn't stop until a beat in the music said so. Then I stomped one foot and pointed my toe as I took off again at a strut. I slung my hair—which was as long as my back—and it whipped around me while I shook my hands as if I was slinging water from them.

I looked up, and a customer was holding out a dollar for me. I walked to his side of the stage and approached him with my garter held out. After he placed the dollar in my garter, I took it out gently over his head and then flicked it back at him as though I didn't need his money. The crowd howled with laughter.

On my last song, I began to slow down and approach the crowd for my tips, greeting each man with a smile as I received my reward. Then a customer who smelled to high heaven stood up to tip me and greet me face to face. Something about him—not just the smell—made my stomach churn, and when he asked me if I would go out with him, I looked him straight in the eye and told him, "Take a bath." He then insulted me like so many others, but I just ignored him.

*What a creep*, I thought to myself. Everything in me didn't like this guy. In spite of the club being dark, I could see the blackheads on his face, and his hair was greasy and his clothes were dingy and smelled like mold. I was all about vanity when I worked, and he appeared as if he had never looked in a mirror.

The next night, the same guy showed up while I was having a drink with another customer. My friend Tammy came to tell me that a man had bought her a drink but was waiting for me.

"Who's waiting?" I asked. She pointed to the guy, and I scoffed. "No way, it's Mr. Nasty."

She went back to the stage bar and sat down with him. But once Tammy left him and I was no longer with a customer, I had no choice but to go see him. My manager would have gone crazy if I left a customer sitting alone when he was there specifically to see me.

I approached him and asked, "Tammy tells me you're

waiting for me?"

"Yes, I want to buy you a drink," he said.

"Okay, let's get a table," I suggested reluctantly.

We found a table near the front door, where the doorman was taking cover charges, and the customer—whose name was Jeffrey—bought me a twenty-dollar drink.

"So what's your name?" he asked.

He was probably expecting a stage name (of which I had plenty), but I told him the truth. "Mary."

He snorted. "Sure it is."

"That's my name!" I insisted.

Although I had spent years going by Cookie, Cherry, and other names, lately I was growing tired of being called something other than who I really was. I had enough identity struggles without juggling multiple names. Besides, it was a good business move because the honesty seemed to win customers over and gain their trust.

"Where do you live?" he asked.

I was honest about this too, at least about the general area where I lived. I even gave customers my home phone number, and when they called, they were usually shocked to find the number wasn't a fake. Most of the time, this led to them returning to Sugar and Spice and buying me drinks, making them the highly valued regulars all dancers craved.

As I sat and talked to Jeffrey, I noticed he had tried to clean up, but the strange smell of his pheromones still hovered around him as if they were trying to warn me about something. Jeffrey said he was a truck driver who lived in the country, and he had recently been divorced and had two kids.

I shared that I too had children and was single but didn't want a relationship because I feared I would be hurt. I used the poor, pitiful me act, talking about my loneliness and struggles with my children to gain his sympathy. The honesty was how I had gotten so many customers to return and spend large amounts of money on me as I led them to believe I needed a man and they might just be the one.

We sat and drank for some time before Jeffrey suggested I just take the money and he would be back the next night. I was shocked and thought, *Who's hustling who here?* There was something...off about him—a whole lot of somethings. He seemed somewhat intelligent but very country, which I didn't like. Under all the crud and oil, he had beautiful eyes, but there was something very desperate behind those eyes. I had never met a man in the clubs who concerned me so much. Flags were jumping up and waving all over the place, but he had left me with a large amount of money. And when it came to money, I was as desperate as he was, so I took it and tried to shake off the creepy feeling he gave me.

The next night, I was back at work again. There was no taking a day off around this time of the month; it was time to come up with money for rent, food, the laundromat, and Nana. When I arrived, I had a bouquet of roses waiting for me from one of my regulars, George. George was one of those who called me at home, and he spent good money whenever he came into Sugar and Spice.

It wasn't uncommon for me to receive roses at work—sometimes three dozen from three different customers at the same time. I asked my customers to do it, partly to make myself feel special or better than I was and partly just to make the other girls jealous and wonder what I had going on with these guys. The funny thing was that I didn't even like roses. At the end of the night when my shift was over, I would give them to the girls or take them home to Nana. I played these games not only with the customers, but also with myself.

I collected the roses George had sent me and then got ready for the night. True to his word, Jeffrey showed up again, but this time, I got forty-dollar drinks and large tips when I went onstage.

After a while, he said, "I know your last name and where you live."

"What?" I asked, confused.

He rattled off my name and address and said, "You really were telling me the truth."

I tried to hide my shock as I asked, "How did you find out?"

He then proceeded to explain that last night after I told him what kind of car I had, he went out to the parking lot and wrote down my license plate number. Then he asked a friend who had access to public information to track down what he could about me. This was long before you could research someone on the Internet, so I couldn't believe he had found out so much about me, especially in so short a time.

I went on playing my game and hustling until I had reached my goal. Now I could pay the bills and have a little more to ride on. But Jeffrey still scared me, and in spite of my street smarts, he was somehow able to get into my head. I thought I had learned every trick and hustle known to the sex industry; but he was already proving me wrong, and this was only the beginning.

*

During this time, my mother had been diagnosed with and was receiving treatment for lung cancer. My father told me that I couldn't bring the babies around her because she was undergoing chemo and her immune system was weak. So although I hadn't seen her much, I talked to her on the phone often, all the while never wanting to believe she would die.

Our relationship had shifted ever so slightly a few years before when Terry and Mary Lynn were about two and a half years old. She enjoyed them very much; you would have never thought she was my mother when she was with them. One day when I came to pick them up from her house, she had fixed little plates of cheese, crackers, and butter for them, and the twins were making a mess with it. I screamed at them and grabbed Mary Lynn by the arm to yell at her for placing her fingers in the butter.

My mother stopped me and looked me in the eye. "Don't treat them the way I treated you," she said.

That was all she needed to say. In those few simple words, my mother admitted to everything I had been through when I was a child. All her terrible mood swings and drunken rages. All the missed meals and neglect. All the love that I had longed for and that she had denied me. From then on, she and I were able to bond as we never had before. And now she was going to die.

It was a slow night at the club, and I was sitting at the main bar watching television, drinking my coffee, and smoking cigarettes. I didn't know why or what came over me, but something told me to go see my mother. She had been in the hospital for more than a month, and I hadn't seen her since Ross was three months old—the first and last time she saw him.

I couldn't shake the feeling that I needed to go, so I asked my manager, Boss, if I could leave early to go see my mother. He was surprised to learn she was in the hospital, as I tried to avoid sharing my personal life in these places, and he was very kind when he told me I could go.

I changed out of my costume into some revealing street clothes and then turned in my drink tickets for the night. I took a cab to the hospital, where at least twenty other friends and family members were all crowded in the waiting room. I hadn't seen some of these folks since childhood, so I spent a few minutes telling everyone where I worked and what I was doing with myself as if it were something worth talking about.

My mother was across the hall hooked up to an IV pole. She had always been petite like me, but today she looked truly small—frail, as I had never seen her.

I approached her bed and said, "Mama, it's Mary. I'm sorry I have so much perfume on; I know it takes your breath." I paused. My mother and I rarely exchanged "I love yous," but that same feeling that brought me here urged me to spit it out. "I just want you to know that I love you."

She then said in a weak voice, "I love you too, Mary. Stop smoking."

The nurse was hooking something to the IV pole connected to my mother, and my aunt started explaining to Mama what she was doing.

"I don't care what they do to me," Mama rasped.

I promised to come back the next day and then called a cab to take me home. Not long after I lay down in bed, the phone rang, and I jumped up in a panic. Somehow I knew what would be waiting for me on the other end of that call.

I picked up the receiver, and it was my sister-in-law. "Mary, your mother died just after you left."

I can't remember if I cried or not. I was just so shocked that I got off the phone as quickly as I could. Something had moved within me to visit my mother that night and tell her I loved her. She had hung on to life long enough to say goodbye to me. Before that night, I had refused to think of my mother's death, but something—God, maybe—had given me the chance to face it so I could see her one last time.

To this day, I have never seen as many people at a funeral as there were at my mother's. I couldn't find a sitter for Ross because most everyone who knew him refused to take him. Unlike the twins, he had received a great deal of attention and got everything he wanted, so he had become a spoiled, hyper, demanding toddler. So I had no choice but to chase him through the funeral home or constantly hold him.

There was no time to grieve, nor did anyone want to see or hear of it. When I got out of the car at the funeral home where my mother's body lay, my knees became weak, but my niece, who was close to my age, turned to me and said, "I don't want to hear you crying." I wasn't sure why she said that, but I sucked up the emotions all the same, as I felt I was doing something wrong.

Once inside, I made my way through the multitude that had shown up. When I entered the room where her body lay, one of my brothers appeared and grabbed my arm. "She is beautiful, Mary," he said, tears streaming down his face. He apparently hadn't gotten the memo about not crying, and everyone was avoiding him.

I shrugged him off and approached the casket to see for myself. There were Valentine cards everywhere, as she had died on Valentine's Day. As my brother had said, my mother was more beautiful than I had ever known her to be. In life, she had always appeared sad and haggard or was drunk and hateful, but now she finally appeared to be at rest. Peace came over me as well now that I knew she was no longer in emotional pain. As strange as it was, I was glad that what she had experienced in this life was over.

After I left the casket, I heard a familiar voice in the hallway. The volume of the crowd increased even more, and everyone started heading for the hallway to see Dirty Dan.

Yes, Dirty Dan had come to pay his respects, and he had a probate from the club with him. They both were drunk and wearing their Vagrant patches. I remained in my chair and watched as everyone followed him into the viewing room like he was some sort of celebrity. He walked up to the casket and placed a marijuana joint and two beers in my mother's casket. I was so embarrassed, but many of my family members thought it was cool.

I hadn't seen Dirty since I was almost twenty years old, and I managed to avoid him that day until we all arrived at the graveyard chapel. Once there, Dirty walked up to me while I held Ross on my hip. Dirty stuck up his middle finger and placed it in my baby's face, and it angered me. Between Ross's hyperactivity, Dirty's crassness, and my inability to mourn at my own mother's funeral, I couldn't come up with much to say to this man who had set my life on this course I was still living.

As everyone started gathering inside the chapel, Dirty said, "This isn't me, Brat. I can't go in a church. I'm gonna go outside and give your ma a salute."

As I sat down in the back row of the church, I realized what he meant by giving my mother a salute. Whenever one of the brothers died, the last thing the Vagrants did before the service ended was line up outside and shoot their guns. The church doors were wide open, and no one but my father and I knew what was about to happen. The whole time during the minister's message, I dreaded what was about to take place but felt helpless to stop it or warn anyone without causing a scene. So when it came time, I just covered Ross's ears and slid down in the bench I was sitting on.

The church was made of concrete, and the gunshots echoed spectacularly throughout the building. Everyone in front of me jumped in surprise, and my baby began to cry. Dirty didn't stop shooting until the clip was empty, and then he collected the empty shell casings and presented them to my father as a keepsake. And that was the last I saw of Dirty Dan for quite some time.

That very night, I returned to work. Everyone knew I had just come from my mother's funeral, but I was determined to stay upbeat and happy, so I chattered to them, saying, "You will never believe after all these years who showed up at my mother's funeral."

"Who?" Boss, my manager, asked.

"Dirty Dan! He read the obituaries and saw my mother's name in the newspaper. It blew me away." Boss just continued to look at me with concern—not the reaction I wanted or was expecting. "I thought he was dead," I explained.

"Are you okay, Mary?" he asked. "Are you sure you want to work tonight?"

"I'm fine. I'll be all right."

So I went through the night working as if nothing had changed, just like my mother would wake up after one of her three-day drunken episodes and act as though nothing ever happened. And so life continued as usual, just another day in the jungle.

# CHAPTER EIGHTEEN

# Hell's Cubbyhole

I continued to dance while Nana watched all three of my children. The money was there and then it wasn't. Our biggest moneymakers were the conventions that brought in a lot of out-of-towners, but even they were beginning to dwindle, bringing in fewer customers who spent less money. Now I was down to depending on a handful of regulars. They showed up maybe twice a month and spent a reasonable amount of money, and any other customers were just strangers who I would never see again but whom I entertained as if I had known them all my life.

Most of all, I was relying on Jeffrey, the customer who had found out my identity and address. I could tell he was beginning to become obsessed with me, but I couldn't shut him down if I wanted to feed my children. I could count on him to buy a few drinks and slip me several hundred dollars on a regular basis.

At the same time, I was becoming closer to George, the man who sent me roses. Between him and Jeffrey, I was keeping my head above water. But unlike Jeffrey, George was a sweet man who seemed to be truly in love with me. They were both truck drivers and vaguely knew one another, but because of their schedules, they never ran into each other at Sugar and Spice. By now, Eric was completely out of my life, and I was becoming lonely and tired of the bar life.

I was even sick of getting tips onstage, which had been the initial appeal of Sugar and Spice. I saw what happened on the nude side of the bar and what girls did for a dollar, which the customers stuck anywhere the girls would allow them. Then the girls would take those dollars to the cashier and exchange them for bigger bills, leaving the smaller bills to circulate among the customers to tip the girls again and again. The same dollar bills circulated night after night, and hand sanitizer wasn't available. It got to the point where I refused to take money from a customer if he wouldn't place it in my garter because I couldn't stop thinking about where that dollar might have been on the nude stage.

I started seeing George outside of the club when I needed to get away from the bar life. He would go with me to take my children to the park, and if I was in need of a friend to loan me cash, George was quick to give me all I needed to take care of my children. Unlike Keith, he never looked down on me for working in the clubs, and he was all around one of the kindest and most trustworthy men I had ever met. Even Nana was okay with him (although her "give it to Jesus" advice still stood).

However, in spite of all of that, I couldn't find it within myself to fall in love with such a nice, harmless guy. I wish I could explain why, but as messed up as I was, I knew what love and passion were, and George was not it.

In sharp contrast to George's sweet interest in me, Jeffrey would flat-out stalk me. George and I often saw him passing my house in his truck, and whenever he came into Sugar and Spice, he would sit with my friend Tammy and stare at me until I became available. Whenever I asked him why he had driven past my house, he gave me some excuse that I never believed. He called me outside of work too, and although I remained cautious, I would talk to him and share bits and pieces about my life.

Once I told him that my car needed a new transmission. Shortly after, he came to the club, I gave him my keys, and he worked on it all night before bringing it back to the club at four in the morning. Not only was the transmission replaced, but a new radio and CD player were installed where the standard radio used to be. He had also changed the oil and detailed it. In spite of all the red flags about him, I was impressed.

Meanwhile, my friend Tammy constantly tried to convince me that Jeffrey was "the one." After sitting with him while he waited for me, she would catch me in the dressing room and tell me that he loved me and that he would be my way out of the clubs. Even more than finding regular customers, this was the true dream of most dancers—to find a man who would provide for them so they could leave this place. However, I told Tammy she was crazy and didn't understand how weird Jeffrey was. Later, after I learned how manipulative Jeffrey could truly be, I wondered if he had convinced her to help persuade me to be with him.

Truth be told, I was getting to the point where a way out of the clubs was all I wanted, even if I didn't agree with Tammy that Jeffrey was the way. I wanted something more for my children, but I didn't know where to turn or what to do with the GED I had earned. Between being a dancer and a mother and so many other things, I felt like I had to be several different people without ever knowing who the real me was. I was sick of seeing my children only a few hours a day since I was gone all night and slept all day to recover. Mary Lynn and

Terry were growing up, and I didn't want them to experience the shame of me dancing, the same type of shame I had known as a child.

One day, after one too many pats on the backside and seeing men do one too many unspeakable acts with rolled-up dollar bills, I decided to stay home for several nights with my babies. The bills were mostly paid, and although I didn't know what would happen after that, I just couldn't stomach going back to that place for a little while.

After a few days, Jeffrey called wanting to know why I hadn't been at the bar. I explained that I was tired of dancing and wanted to be with my babies. I hesitated for a moment but then mentioned that the rent was due soon and I was broke. Although I was afraid of him, I knew all I had to do was say the word and he would bring the money to me. And sure enough, as soon as I mentioned my money troubles, he was all too willing to come by and be my savior.

I knew he knew where I lived, so there was no need to tell him my address, but now that I was giving him permission to come, I realized I didn't want him around my children. So first, I asked him to leave the money under the floor mat of my car, but he was offended by that. Finally, I decided he could come over as long as he sat outside with me while the children played in the grass in front of the apartment.

The children and I were already outside when Jeffrey showed up that evening. He handed me three hundred dollars, and I felt awkward but took it anyway. We then sat on the steps while my children played in the grass, and I enjoyed watching them wrestle and run in circles. Once the children were worn out, I took them inside and put them to bed, but I still didn't welcome Jeffrey in and instead left him outside on the steps. Then I joined him again while leaving the door open so I could listen for my children.

We talked for a while, and for the first time, I started to feel relaxed and comfortable with him. Now that some time had passed since my first smelly encounter with him, I realized he was actually handsome in his way, with a beautiful smile (if you could get him to smile). He had sky-blue eyes with thick lashes, and he was muscular and tanned from time in the sun. I wondered why I had never seen this side of him in the club. Through our conversation, I also discovered he was extremely intelligent. This was something I had always admired in a man because I wanted to be with someone I could learn from.

That night, the only red flag that came up was Jeffrey's opinion of my children, especially my boys. He said they were out of control and I treated them differently. It made me angry—my children were none of his business, after all—but if I was honest with myself, I knew he was right. Ross was hard to control, and I enabled his misbehavior by giving him whatever he wanted. If he cried and threw a fit, I gave him a piece of candy, not realizing I was rewarding his bad behavior. I had been so strict with the twins that I wanted to make up for my mistakes with Ross. I had failed to do so much with them that I thought by bonding with Ross, perhaps I could bond with my twins and finally get it right.

Over the next several days, Jeffrey and I chatted on the phone, and he made me laugh as I never had with him before. I again didn't understand why I hadn't seen his sense of humor or other attractive qualities after months of seeing him at Sugar and Spice. The next weekend, he brought his own children to my apartment, and they were very well behaved. He didn't allow them to make a ruckus even while my children ran wild through the house showing off in front of his children.

We were becoming close fast. Jeffrey continued to pay my

bills and saw to it that my children and I had anything and everything we could want or need. I finally began to see what Tammy had seen all this time—that he really did love me and that with him, I might be able to have the life I longed for away from the clubs. The red flags were dropping away, and I was beginning to fall in love as I never had with George. But the final red flag was still to come, as I hadn't yet seen the conditions Jeffrey lived in when he was away from me and the club.

*

Jeffrey lived in the country on ten acres of waist-deep weeds. It was the same country town that Dirty and I had lived in without heat or water. I loved the country and didn't have any ill feelings about this little town, but in the years that followed, it would come to haunt me just as strongly as the red light district and the sound of Harley Davidsons roaring through the streets.

But that was all still far in the future when Jeffrey took me to his house for the first time. Our kids were with sitters, so it was just the two of us driving down the dark, winding country road that night. We finally reached an A-frame house, and in the pitch darkness, the lights from inside the house made it look as though it had eyes. We pulled into the long dirt driveway and trod through the tall grass on our way to his house. There were no streetlights like in the city, or even a porch light to guide our way.

I was frightened of snakes, so Jeffrey took my hand as we waded through the weeds. The porch steps—or what was left of them—were made of rotten, broken boards, and the porch itself was mostly gone, leaving a gaping hole where the threshold should have been. Two boards acted as a plank for us to walk across to get into the house. The front door was a sliding glass door, and windows that were the exact size of the door stood on either side. Two more windows stood on top of them, making the entire front of the house glass.

When Jeffrey slid the door open (with some effort, since it was partially off its track), I was immediately assaulted by the stench. It was a familiar smell, and it took me a moment to realize it was the mold and must I had smelled on Jeffrey the night we met—only a hundredfold stronger.

He turned on a dim light, and we walked through the living room into the kitchen. Dirty dishes completely covered the countertop and looked like they had been there for months. Every bug known to man was buzzing around the kitchen, likely due to the bags of smelly garbage that littered the floor.

Directly off the kitchen was a deck that was filled with even more garbage. Jeffrey's bedroom was a loft over the kitchen that you could reach only by climbing a twenty-foot aluminum ladder in the living room. The living room itself was at least three stories high. The walls were made of natural wood, and some sort of plant or mold was growing on the walls. Pornography and nude photographs of women were strewn all over the couch, and Jeffrey made a pitiful attempt to hide them when we entered the room.

I asked if I could use the bathroom, and the reek only got worse in there. The lime buildup in the commode looked sickening, and there was a large, square opening in the floor where stairs led down to the basement and laundry room. When I flushed the commode, a well pump kicked on and a squealing noise came from the basement.

When I came out of the bathroom, Jeffrey had turned on another light, which allowed me to see the baby field mouse that had gotten caught in the shag carpet. He picked it up and threw it out the door. Poison ivy had made its way through the cracks in the wall into the house and was growing up the beautiful wood walls.

Jeffrey appeared to be embarrassed, and I knew the shame he was feeling. At different times in my life, I had lived with roaches and drunks and lived without heat and sanitation. I tried to make him feel better by assuring him that I had lived in worse conditions—though this was only partially true. This house needed a complete transformation. It was another red flag that I left at half-staff.

From the first time I met him, there was something about Jeffrey that was trying to warn me to stay away, and his house was a monument-sized reminder of that warning. But like so many times before, I didn't listen to or trust my heart. My heart had been disappointed and beaten up so many times that I didn't believe it anymore.

Besides, Jeffrey promised to take care of me so that I would no longer have to work in the industry, and despite his poor qualities, I had no reason to doubt him in this area. Even outside of the clubs, he had been financially caring for my children and me when no one ever had. Where I had always paid for everything with Dirty Dan and Keith, Jeffrey went above and beyond to meet my needs—not the other way around.

My desperation to be free from the bars and the sex industry was stronger than my first impression of Jeffrey. Maybe Tammy was right in telling me that he was my way out. Maybe with his help, I could be the mother I had never had as a child.

Shortly after this night, I called George to inform him that I was now with Jeffrey and couldn't see him anymore. George respected my decision to break up with him, but he was deeply concerned that I was seeing Jeffrey. He knew of Jeffrey through other truck drivers, and he told me he was strange and warned me to be careful with him.

*What could possibly be worse than my life with Dirty Dan?* I thought. In spite of everyone's warnings, I decided to move in with Jeffrey because I thought the country would be good for the children. Once I was out of the club, I could finally be the mother that I longed to be, and I would finally have someone to support me and relieve some of my stress as I saw my daughter through surgery after surgery. And I would finally get some sleep and maybe even pursue my dream of going to college.

But before I would take my babies to this man's house, I bought every cleaning product on the market and had Jeffrey haul off the trash to the incinerator. I pulled up poison ivy from inside the house and placed newspaper in the cracks to prevent the weeds from growing through the shifted foundation. The glass that covered the entire front of the house leaked when it rained, and there was no placing pans to catch the rain as the water ran down the inside of the glass doors and damaged the floor. I attempted to repair them by caulking the areas that had moved away from the frame of the windows.

I did everything possible to make it a home, and Jeffrey cut down the fields so the children could play on the swings I had bought. Once I got upstairs to the bedroom, the heat was unbearable, as there was no window for ventilation, and that was when I discovered jars of urine stuffed in a corner. I gagged while removing them and never mentioned it to Jeffrey.

I bought lamps and lumber for the porch and the deck. Jeffrey built a landing and steps to the bedroom, and he put up walls for bedrooms in the basement for my children. As hard and disgusting as all the work was, I felt I was finally reaching the light at the end of the tunnel that was the sex industry.

This man had promised me the world and everything in it, and I believed him. Nana would have said to give it to Jesus, but I was giving it all to Jeffrey and not looking back. I believed that I could sweep my past under a rug and finally breathe freely now that I had survived the worst.

However, everything that I had survived in my past would not top this man and the horrors he would bring into my life for the next decade.

# CHAPTER NINETEEN

# Happy Family

The big day came, and I moved into Jeffrey's house with my children. The whole house had a fresh coat of paint, most of the floors had been replaced, the walls had been bleached, and the bathroom was brand new. It was hard to believe, but hell's cubbyhole had transformed into a cute farmhouse fit for a family like mine. The children and I had given Jeffrey a reason to make something of it, and after all our hard work, we were ready to be the family I had never had growing up.

It was 1990, and I would soon be thirty years old. I had worked in the sex industry for the better part of fifteen years. My twins were going into the third grade, and Ross was around three years old. I was happy as I hadn't been in a long time, and I loved the house that Jeffrey now called ours.

For a long while, things were normal. Jeffrey and I spent most of our days looking after the children together and enjoying country living. My family members visited often, and every Sunday, we gathered with Jeffrey's extended family at his parents' house for dinner. Although his family had their own problems, I felt comfortable and welcome, and my heart was full when I watched the children play games together.

When Jeffrey was around his family, the way he talked and his entire personality changed. He adopted a drawling country accent, and he was louder and more boisterous than he was with us. But once we got home, he was the person I had met in the bar—solemn and sad.

At these dinners, I learned that Jeffrey's father had drunk heavily all of his life just like my mother and that he had abused Jeffrey when he was a child. In fact, I never knew his father to be sober. His father talked down to his mother, and she carried out his every demand. You could hear him yell from the living room, and she would hurry to him to meet his needs. She was a Christian woman who believed a wife should be obedient to her husband. I felt sorry for her, but I wasn't intimidated by such circumstances; I had been around alcoholics and people with issues all my life, so I felt I fit in.

Shortly before we moved in, Jeffrey had crushed his foot in an accident with a forklift. While he fought for workers' compensation, he was home with the children and me 24/7. At first, I enjoyed this because Jeffrey was so helpful with the children that I felt I finally had a partner in caring for them. But then hints of his father slowly began to reveal themselves.

First it was in the way he started to control the people I saw and when I saw them. Most of my friends and family lived very far away, so after a few months, their visits dropped off and I wanted to go see them. The children and I were getting lonely and feeling the emptiness of the fields surrounding us. But Jeffrey became very agitated when I talked about going to the city, and he forbade us to go without him—not that he went often. The house I had worked so hard to make a home was starting to feel like a prison, and now that I was no longer working, I didn't have the means to release us.

The cabin fever led to many arguments—mostly over the

children. Jeffrey started writing down lists of rules that he expected both me and the children to follow. And since he didn't have a job to occupy his time, he instead spent his energies planning out our days in fifteen-minute increments, including when we were to use the bathroom. He made the children finish everything on their plates even if it made them sick, so I began putting less on their plates to try to shield them (and myself) from the daily anguish at mealtimes.

In response to Jeffrey's strictness, I didn't have much of a regimen or structure for us. The more he attempted to control us, the less I would expect of my children, which I'm sure confused them.

Even my beautiful house wasn't living up to all my hopes. We depended on well water, and whenever it ran out, we couldn't take baths or had to share bathwater. I would let the baby wash first, then Mary Lynn, then Terry, and then me. I couldn't wash clothes, and I often flushed the commode and mopped the floors with leftover bathwater. In the summer, the heat was unbearable as the sun beat down on the glass windows that took up the entire front of the house. In the winter, we used kerosene heaters throughout the house, but the basement where my children slept was extremely cold and the kerosene heaters couldn't keep up. Still, Jeffrey refused to let them sleep upstairs.

In addition, the heaters were very old and dangerous, as Jeffrey rigged them himself to make them work. The fumes made us sick as the carbon monoxide poison made its way to the top of the loft, where there was no ventilation. The basement had only one window, and I lay awake at night imagining a fire breaking out and my children being unable to get out of the house. So I got up often to check on them throughout the night, and I coached them on how to escape if there was a fire.

My own flaws with my children continued as I paid Ross an abundance of attention while neglecting Mary Lynn and Terry. But now I had Jeffrey around to point out this flaw constantly and use it to degrade and manipulate me. He became jealous of my own son and would say, "You love your kids more than you love me" to try to turn my attention and affection toward him.

That should have been the last straw—after all, how dare he put himself in competition with my children?—but this only scratched the surface of his mental abuse. Like Keith, Jeffrey reminded me constantly of where I had come from and told me that my people were white trash. When I was at my lowest, he drilled me with questions about my past and then later used what I told him against me, to try to convince me that I needed him because only he could love me in spite of all my flaws.

All the red flags were turning out to be accurate. Although I wish I could say this drove me away, to be honest, part of me believed that what he said was true. When you hear the person you're closest to confirm all the worst things you think about yourself, you lose the strength to think you can do anything to change your life—even if you had that kind of strength in the first place. I knew I was depressed, and when he told me I had mental problems, how could I argue? I certainly felt crazy between his control and the conditions of the house. I already struggled with self-doubt and the lowest of self-esteem, and he took every opportunity to convince me I couldn't trust myself and my decision making.

Although I was with my children daily like I had longed for, the depression was driving me to become more and more like my mother. I kept the house dark and slept all day and stayed up all night while my children slept. One moment, I would be very excited and upbeat, but within the hour, I would become sad and question myself and everything about my life. Although I had seen a therapist, I refused to take medication because it reminded me of the addicts in my family. I started to long to go back to Sugar and Spice so I could support my children and be free of Jeffrey.

But none of the control and mental abuse could compare to Jeffrey's sexual deviance, which began to present itself shortly after I moved in with him. I learned later that it's called *voyeurism*, but I just referred to it as "sick sex." It started with him wanting to watch porn with me. I had had enough of pornography to last me a lifetime, so I refused. I couldn't get him to understand why, so he just moved on to asking me to record us having sex. Each request became more bizarre, twisted, and warped, and despite everything I had witnessed working in the sex industry, even I wasn't equipped to handle all he threw at me.

Jeffrey came up with outlandish requests such as wife swapping and me sleeping with other men while he watched. I flat-out refused, of course, but he brought up these things constantly, sometimes begging and other times trying to convince me why they were a good idea. We got into heated arguments over it, and he would keep me up all night and follow me around the house if I tried to walk away.

"You did it for Dirty Dan, and you're going to do it for me," he would say.

Although I felt there was some truth to what he was saying, I argued back, "No! Dirty didn't ask me to sleep with men while he watched."

"I know what women do in motorcycle gangs," he insisted. "You were nothing more than their whore, but you're my whore now and you'll do what I say."

The only way I got any relief was to tell Jeffrey stories of what I had done with other men. He would ask me what their genitals looked like and other details of our encounters, and then he would pleasure himself while I sat on the edge of the bed and told dirty stories. Whenever I gave in to him like this, I would disassociate myself and see my body from the other side of the room as I sat on the side of the bed. It was a literal out-of-body experience as I watched myself say these things that my rational mind never would.

Jeffrey had a way of breaking me down, but he couldn't break me to the point of actually doing any of the sick acts he wanted. In fact, I would say, "A Vagrant couldn't break me; you think I'll let you?"

I honestly thought I had been through it all, but Jeffrey was proving me wrong. Eventually, I gave him an ultimatum: Either we go to couples therapy or it's over. I believed anyone could change. I knew he had had a rough childhood just like I had, and therapy had helped me, so I thought it could help him too.

But it was all just a game to him. After a few heated sessions, my therapist refused to see Jeffrey anymore because they got into such an intense argument over the children. They were literally on the edge of their seats, almost face to face as they shouted. He knew how to push people's buttons, and my therapist was no exception. He could talk you to death and justify everything he did. I was exhausted by his relentlessness and felt hopeless after even my therapist lost it with him.

Therapy had been my last best hope, and when that didn't work, I was convinced that life would have been better for all of us if I had stayed in the strip clubs. So I packed up the children and left the house I had worked so hard to revive, and we moved into a trailer to be near one of my sisters. Then it was back to Sugar and Spice to make sure I would not have to depend on Jeffrey for money, because that was his main way of controlling us.

However, money at the bars was as up and down as ever, especially now that I had lost many of my old regulars. Jeffrey knew this, and when times got desperate, there would be a knock at the door, and there he would stand with toys for the children and gifts for me, so that it felt rude not to invite him in. At Christmas, he showed up with a thousand dollars for me because he knew I spoiled my children during this time and hated to see them do without. He was slowly working his way back in, trying to show that he had changed and promising things would be different if I would only come back to him.

I felt as if there were nowhere to run, nowhere to hide from this man. He knew where I worked, knew where I lived, knew how to get in touch with me. And if I held him off on one front, he would just find another. It was as if one of the demons from my dreams had come alive to chase me for real.

For example, one time Jeffrey kept me on the phone for three hours trying to convince me to come back to him. Over and over I said, "We can't make it, Jeffrey. It's not going to work; you won't change." I knew if I hung up, he would just call back repeatedly, or if I took the phone off the hook, he would just come out to the trailer.

But I could take only so much of him trying to get into my head before I finally hung up and took the phone off the hook. Sure enough, an hour later Jeffrey was at the door making a scene while my children were trying to sleep. As I was trying to get him to leave, he took out a glass soda bottle and smacked himself in the head with it.

Horrified and scared, I ran to my sister's trailer and told her what was going on. She returned with me to my trailer and (saint that she was) began to pick the glass out of Jeffrey's head so his wounds wouldn't become infected.

I was suddenly taken back to when I had first moved in with him, when he crushed his foot with a forklift. Had that truly been an accident? Or was it his way of ensuring that he would be with me all the time and control my every move? I wouldn't have believed it before, but now that I had seen him hurt himself with my own eyes, I was beginning to understand just how far he was willing to go to come after me.

Terrified, I told him that if he would just go home, I would be with him again, as long as I could stay where I was living with the children. I would have said anything to get him away from me and my children in that moment, and I resolved to figure out a way to escape for good.

This promise didn't buy me much time, however. Shortly after the soda bottle incident, Jeffrey called me, and I said, as clearly and boldly as I could, "It's over between us, Jeffrey. We can never be together."

"I'll kill myself," he said, and to my shock, I heard a gun being cocked. "I swear to God, I'll do it." These last words were mumbled, as he clearly had the gun in his mouth.

So this was it. He had played his final card, the one he knew would beat me where presents and begging had failed. I had spent my childhood thinking if I could just keep the drunks calm and peaceful, my parents would love and care for me. I had spent my teenage years and early twenties thinking I was responsible for the abuse I took from a biker and then my children's father. If I was just a better ol' lady, if I wasn't such a whore, I wouldn't deserve what was happening to me. And now if this man took his life, it would be my fault.

So I went back to Jeffrey. Since there was no getting away from him, I felt like I was stuck with him, and since I felt I deserved no better, I couldn't imagine a better life for myself and my children.

# CHAPTER TWENTY

# Educating a Stripper

The one bright spot of being with Jeffrey was that it allowed me to finally go back to school. Now that I had my GED, my therapist directed me to Vocational Rehabilitation. I underwent many psychological and career placement tests, and in the end, my education counselor suggested I learn how to program and process computers. I wanted to learn how to become a writer, but I was used to allowing everyone else to think for me, so when my counselor said I would do well in a clerical computer job, I felt I had no choice but to go to the school she chose for me.

Shortly before beginning school, I discovered I was pregnant with a baby girl. Jeffrey had sworn he would try to be normal and would be easier on the children, and now more than ever, I wanted to believe him.

I had worked all through my pregnancies with my other children, and this time would be no different—except instead of a bar, I would be in the classroom. The children went to daycare and summer activities with Nana while I spent my days going to school. Jeffrey soon followed my example since he couldn't drive a truck after crushing his foot and needed to find a new career. He was extremely smart and would help me with my homework. He saw that computers were becoming the way of the future, so he modeled what I had done and went through school to become a programmer.

While Jeffrey had an easy time with school, I was intimidated from day one. It was a small school that had just opened its doors. The pristine new classroom looked overwhelming to a poor girl like me who felt like she didn't belong in a place with such nice things. Rows of computers, enough for perhaps sixty students, seemed to shout at me that I could never succeed here.

On that first day, the instructor stood before the blackboard, introduced herself, and handed out a piece of paper that she called a syllabus. As I wedged my growing belly under the computer, I squinted at the paper and felt every muscle in my body tense up.

*I can't even type, and what's a syllabus?* I thought to myself. Words that I had never seen were splattered across the paper, and I was terrified. I couldn't understand it, and I wanted to run out and scream and cry. But I stayed in my seat and hoped the day would end quickly so I could breathe. I watched the other students as they wrote in their notebooks while the teacher talked, and I thought to myself, *Should I be doing that too?*

It was eight hours a day, five days a week, just like a real job. I did everything I could to keep up, but I couldn't comprehend the computer language. Even the school's staff was convinced that I would fail. For the first four months, I cried and cried and carried my books home to study alongside my children as they did their homework. I was attempting to learn computer language when I still couldn't read the daily newspaper properly.

Pregnancy was making me hormonal, and life with Jeffrey

was making me depressed. As I should have known they would, things were starting to fall apart. One night in my third trimester, Jeffrey shoved me when I was standing at the top of the steps, but I caught myself before I fell and thought he wouldn't dare do anything like that again while I was carrying his child. But then the next night, we got into a heated argument over the children, and he slung me to the floor. My ribs slammed into the edge of the coffee table, narrowly missing the baby in my womb. Jeffrey's only response was to snarl, "Get your fat a—— up."

It was time to go again. I felt I couldn't call the police because we were in a very small town where everyone, including the authorities, knew Jeffrey and would take his side. I had no choice but to go to Louisville and go back to the spouse abuse center. I was ashamed to be back again because of yet another abuser who had come into my life. But I was pregnant, broke, and scared and thought this was my only hope.

It was hard not to feel like I was going through the same cycle again as I went through the same routine and was given the same resources and the same counselor. My one encouragement was that when I told my counselor about Jeffrey's sick sex, she said that it was rare for a woman to refuse a man like Jeffrey because such men were usually able to break women down to the point that they gave in and surrendered to it.

I was relieved to find out that I wasn't the only one who had experienced abuse like this. I thought that people in the normal world didn't deal with such things and that freaks and perverts were only in the clubs and peep shows. How naïve of me; after all I had seen and been through, I should have known better. I had assumed that once I got away from Dirty Dan and Keith, I would be safe and never have to live the life of a victim again. But of all of them, I felt Jeffrey was by far the worst.

At the end of our session, my counselor mentioned, "If you go into labor while you're here in the shelter, we will have to place your children in the Home of the Innocents while you're in the hospital."

"Hell no, you won't!" I all but shouted.

Surprised, she said, "It's just until you get out of the hospital."

"No! I will find another way."

So history began to repeat itself again as I started looking for a place to live just weeks before giving birth, just as I had with Ross. I was terrified that if my children went into foster care while I was in the hospital, I would lose them forever. That very day, I went back to my old neighborhood and walked up and down the streets trying to find a place available to rent. Every now and then I would have a pain and would stop on the sidewalk to breathe through it and tell my baby, "Hold on, baby girl. Mama's got to get us a home before you can be born, so stay put."

Finally, after several days of searching, I found a small shotgun house that had four rooms and a backyard for the children to play in. I called the woman who owned the house and pleaded with her, telling her that as soon as I got back on my feet, I could pay the rent. Even though I had put school on hold and didn't have a job, I knew I could still hustle money in the bars. I cried and begged this woman to rent to me, and she finally agreed.

Within days, I moved in, and now that I didn't have the locks and curfews of the women's shelter to protect me, Jeffrey tracked me down. He brought me furniture and dishes that I had left at his house. I didn't want him coming around at all, or at least hoped that he would drop off all my belongings in one trip, but he used our possessions as an excuse to keep coming back and forth.

Within two days of living in the house, I went into labor in the middle of the night. Jeffrey went with me to the hospital and was with me the whole time I was delivering. However, there was tension in the delivery room because the doctor who delivered my baby girl was the same one who had examined me after Jeffrey pushed me into the table and bruised my ribs. When Tara came into the world, the doctor refused to let Jeffrey hold her and was rude and short with him since he knew Jeffery was the perpetrator. The entire staff was aware of what Jeffrey had done, and the doctor informed Adult Protective Services that he was there.

In response, I was issued a social worker who started visiting my house on a weekly basis. In the past, I would have found this intimidating, but I didn't mind these days. The social worker was supportive, and I added her to my team of professionals who helped me to get back in school and protect my children.

Three months after Tara was born in April of 1992, I placed her in daycare and went back to finish school. I was so worried that someone would hurt my children that I would leave the house early to spend time with the daycare workers. As with Nana, I made certain to befriend anyone who cared for my children and got to know them personally to ensure my babies were safe.

In school, I was finally beginning to catch on. Before long, I would be one of the top students in the class, and at the Computer Education Services graduation in March of 1994, I received an award for excellence. I truly didn't know why I was being honored, but the fact that I had been failing and then shot up seemed to impress everyone. Still, I felt awkward accepting the award and gave the credit to my therapist.

Next, I set my sights on the University of Louisville. My dreams had evolved into wanting to study psychology. After years of going to therapy, I wanted to learn for myself everything to do with the human psyche and maybe figure myself out along the way.

My increased interest in psychology probably also grew out of my feelings that I myself was going crazy. Jeffrey never allowed me to have a stable life with my children as he continued his relentless pursuit of me. He continued to call until I took the phone off the hook, or he would drive the forty miles from his house to mine just to creep up and down the street like he used to when I was dating George. He would call my voicemail and try hundreds of number combinations until he figured out my password so he could keep an eye on what I was doing and to whom I was talking. Whenever I tried to argue with him, he told me that *I* was the crazy one because I had come from crazy people, and that I owed him and it wasn't fair that I had done so much for Dirty Dan but wasn't willing to do it for him.

I kept him at bay as best I could and refused to move back to his farmhouse. But every once in a while, I got exhausted and let him back into our lives, only to kick him out again once the sick sex and control reared their ugly heads. He always said the same thing: "I promise I'll stop asking you to do things you don't want to do. Just come back to me. Nobody will ever love you like I do." Although I had plenty of evidence to the contrary, I wanted to believe him, and he had an extra foothold on me in Tara, as I wanted at least one of my children to have her father.

Now that I had a social worker investigating his abuse, Jeffrey no longer put his hands on me or left a bruise that would be apparent. Instead, he made threats such as, "I'll chop you up into little pieces and put you in the well. No one will ever find you." He preyed upon my childhood insecurities and fears that the authorities would not believe me and would separate me from my children if I went to them about Jeffrey.

I had no doubt he was capable of everything he threatened, and I truly believed that I was safest if I was at least communicating with him and knew what he was doing and thinking. It would have been far worse to try to disappear only to have him show up angrier and more determined than ever.

With all this stress, I began to suffer from panic attacks and acute anxiety. I sometimes didn't eat for days at a time, and my teeth would chatter and my whole body would shake uncontrollably as if it were the middle of winter. Even my hair began to fall out. My therapist suggested I take medication, but I knew no medicine could cure what was going on.

That all changed one night when the panic attacks became more severe than ever. A rash had broken out all over my body, and I couldn't stop pacing. The same song had been playing in my head for a week, and I was convinced, however irrationally, that I was going to die. I had called my therapist all day to tell her that I was afraid but didn't know why, and left her message after rambling message. I had let Jeffrey run me over the edge, and I was becoming as obsessive as he was.

Finally, after hours of hysteria and calling my therapist all through the night, she answered the phone and asked in a sleepy voice, "Will you admit yourself to the hospital, Mary?"

Thankfully, my children were with Nana, and I answered, "Yes, anything, just help me."

My therapist arrived at five in the morning and wrapped a blanket around my shoulders since I couldn't stop shaking. She then took me to her office and began to call different hospitals. Later that afternoon, I was admitted to a psychiatric ward for evaluation. I lay in the bed all night unable to sleep because every sound was amplified. Colors were brighter than normal, and the unfamiliar smells of the hospital were heightened too. And above all, I worried for my children, knowing I had to get it together for them. After a while, a nurse came in and gave me a shot to sedate me, and for the first time in a month, I experienced some relief from the chaos of my mind.

It took two weeks and a tiny little pill to bring me back from my mental torment. Once I was home, I knew Jeffrey had to go for good. I stood strong and told him I had had enough and he wasn't going to change himself or change me. Predictably, this did not work, and he continued to call day after day, spouting his promises, threats, arguments, and pleading.

But even worse than threats of suicide, Jeffrey's new trump card on me was Tara. One particular night after I had talked to him for hours, he started telling me that he would take Tara away from me. I feared he could actually do it now that he could use the fact that I had been in the mental hospital and had been a prostitute in the past.

So just to appease him, I told him I would think about getting back together if he would just let me go to sleep. Finally, at about one in the morning, I got off the phone, checked on the children, and collapsed into bed.

About an hour and a half later, I woke to the sound of someone crying next to my bed. Thinking it was one of the children, I opened my eyes—only to see a grown man standing over me.

"Jeffrey!" I screamed. "What are you doing here?"

"I burned my foot," he answered.

Still startled and trying to wake up, I squinted down at his foot as he lifted it up toward me. The entire bottom of his foot was blistered, and burned carpet was smashed into his wounded flesh. I almost gagged at the sight.

"Why didn't you go to the hospital?" I demanded. "Or your family? Why did you drive all the way out here?"

"I need you," was his only reply.

I knew right then what he had done, but there was no proving it and I knew no one would believe me. He had hurt himself yet again to try to win my attention and sympathy. I must have left the front door unlocked, and with his foot in such bad shape, I couldn't bring myself to kick him out, even if I could have physically removed him.

So I had him lay down in my bed and left to fetch a cold compress for his foot. My children woke up and were surprised to find Jeffrey there since they had heard me tell him over the phone for hours that he couldn't come back.

For three days, he refused to go to the hospital or even leave my bed. I spent my days monitoring his blisters and soaking his foot trying to get the carpet out until I finally convinced him to have his foot looked at, hoping he would get better and go home.

The doctor said Jeffrey still needed to be off his feet for a while, so it was back to my house now that he had the excuse that he was injured and needed me. I couldn't help but feel that we were stuck with him for good, but what happened next would give me hope that he could finally be the man I had always hoped he would be.

# CHAPTER TWENTY-ONE

# Finding God in the Crazy

While Jeffrey was recovering, my brother Richard stopped by the house to tell me he was attending a church and wanted me to go with him. I was happy that Richard had turned his life around since getting out of prison for murder, but I had no interest in going to church or listening to his newfound religion.

However, Jeffrey found a new friend in my brother and actually listened to him with respect, unlike his interactions with me or anyone else in our lives. Before I met him, Jeffrey had been a member of a Pentecostal church and had read a great deal of the Bible. He agreed to go to one of Richard's church services, and my brother demanded that I attend as well. I figured this was another one of Jeffrey's plans to work his way back in, and with his pleading promise that he would not force his sick sex on me, I agreed to go to church with Jeffrey to please my brother.

The church was in a storefront building and had perhaps ten members who sat on metal folding chairs they had arranged on the old wooden floors. Services began at ten in the morning, which was very early for me since I usually stayed up all night and slept during the day. But I pulled myself out of bed not knowing what to expect. The service began with old gospel hymns. The minister's wife played a keyboard while a young man played a box guitar and his girlfriend sang "Amazing Grace."

I sat as far back from the pulpit as I could. I stood when the members stood and sat when they sat, not knowing what else to do. Although I understood very little of what was going on or what the pastor said, I was humbled to see the vulnerability of people crying out to God. It reminded me of a time at my stepmother's church when my father went up to the pulpit after the service to have people pray over him. Although he always carried a handkerchief like the ones I was diapered in as a baby, I rarely saw him use it, least of all to wipe away tears. But on that day, tears were streaming down his face so fast and so hard that I wondered what the pastor had said to hurt my daddy.

I went home that day as a teenager full of questions that never got answered. Later, I pieced together that my father had taken a lifetime of sin and pain up to the altar that day, and his tears were for the overwhelming love and forgiveness he felt upon confessing his sins.

Whenever my mother had talked about God, she always focused on what God could do to you, not what he could do for you, and now that I was in my thirties, I was beginning to see the difference. Yes, God hated sin and had wrath for unrepentant sinners as the fiery minister in my stepmother's church had preached. But I didn't need anyone to tell me I was a sinner bound for hell. I already knew that I was flawed and broken; the feeling of hopelessness I carried with me every day was proof of that.

But what I didn't know was that there was more to God than the image of the scary judge that had been shouted at me when I was a child. As the pastor in that tiny storefront church explained, God also provided a way out of sin and wrath by offering forgiveness through Jesus Christ. God knew there would always be sinners like Dirty Dan and Jeffrey and even me, but instead of blasting us all to hell like we deserved, he came to Earth as a man, Jesus, died on the cross to pay for our sins, and then rose to life again so that we too could have life in him.

I knew what it was like to live under the burden of my own and others' sins, and I knew what it was like to live in fear of God's wrath for all the terrible things I had done. Those were the things God could do to me, but now I was beginning to see that what God could do for me was to teach me a love and forgiveness I had never known. Something about what was said in the church that day made me feel like God was whispering to me, "See, Mary, ALL can be forgiven."

My heart became consumed with love, and a strange peace descended on me where I stood. I knew it was nothing I was conjuring up in my own mind because I did not come here looking for anything but a way to appease my family. There was a sense of hope and rest that I couldn't see or touch, but that I could feel all the same. I hungered for more, a hunger that would remain with me from that day forward.

By the end of the service, I was hooked and was convinced that God was Jeffrey's only hope of changing and becoming the man I had wanted him to be way back when I first moved into his house. Before that day, I would have thought that Jeffrey was the only one who needed God, but now I saw my need for forgiveness too. All of Nana's advice over the years finally clicked in my brain; if we just gave our problems to God, we could be rescued from our demons—me from my anxiety and him from his voyeurism.

Jeffrey agreed with me, and we started attending every service until he had a problem with the pastor and wanted to go somewhere else. I didn't care though. I was just thrilled that he was now at least looking for answers to our problems. I truly thought Jeffrey wanted to change, and I was willing to go to any church where he could learn.

A few years before, an ex-Vagrant named Billy had found Jesus and left the biker gang. He and his ol' lady were now married and were living their lives for the Lord. Billy was even pastoring a church. I was shocked when Jeffrey asked me about going to Billy's church, but after one service and a great conversation with Billy, Jeffrey and I joined his church. Many of the people in this church had been arrested for drugs or other offenses but had overcome many sins to be truly born again. I felt I fit in there and didn't have to hide anything among such a loving and giving community.

It wasn't long before I would love the church and the teachings and love of Jesus. I read my Bible on a daily basis and learned to pray and give all my needs to God. Jeffrey had stopped his sexual deviance, and my children were happy. I was the happiest I had ever been, and I told anyone who would listen about my newfound love for Christ. I felt that I no longer needed worldly counsel, so I cut all ties with the professionals who had been helping me with my life and my children.

For the first time in my life, I felt I was free and could sense the presence of God in our lives. Nana was so proud. With each church service, I would cry even though I didn't know why, and whenever the elders stood in front of the pews after service, I would get in line for prayer. In his sermons, Billy talked about his days as a Vagrant and told stories that I could relate to. I finally felt as if I belonged somewhere that was good and decent.

But it wouldn't be long before I started to feel guilty that Jeffrey and I were living together but weren't married. It had been months since he had burned his foot, and I wanted to forget all about the past and everything we had been through. He was involved with people who were a good influence on our lives, and we weren't isolated any longer. I felt we had a chance with God in our lives, so we set a date to marry and shortly after the wedding moved back to the country to try and make it a home once again.

By now, Jeffrey was programming computers for a company and was making good money compared to his days as a truck driver. I had been working in the office of a health food store but had been fired because I couldn't keep up. We didn't need the money anyway, so I became a full-time mother—the one thing I had wanted since the children were born.

Every morning, I got Jeffrey ready for work and the children off to school. I listened to Charles Stanley and Christian music and read my Bible while doing housework. I couldn't wait to attend church on Wednesdays and Sundays and didn't mind traveling back and forth from the country to attend any functions the church had.

One Sunday, the church announced that it was hosting a marriage retreat, and I was thrilled to attend it with Jeffrey. Nana agreed to keep the children while we went on the trip. Although Nana was pleased that I had found God, she was still not sure about Jeffrey. But we were doing well and had a lot to celebrate in our life and marriage. I packed my Bible and notebooks and something cute to wear to bed. Since we had been going to church, Jeffrey hadn't asked me once to do anything that made me feel uncomfortable, and I truly felt he had changed.

On the way to the retreat, we were driving down the road

listening to music, and I was beyond happy. I hadn't been on a trip since my ill-fated adventure out west with Dirty's sister. As we talked, Jeffrey told me he had a present for me and I should look in the bag in the glove compartment.

I opened the compartment and reached in excitedly. However, when I pulled out the bag, I found that it contained sex toys—not one, but two. My heart sank.

Here I had uprooted my children again, and with this one sign, I knew the cycle was going to start all over, ending with me leaving him yet again. Jeffrey tried to convince me that all the couples at the retreat did these sorts of things and that I was being a prude. But my heart was broken, and once we arrived at the hotel, I went straight to our room. I didn't want to look at anyone for fear that they would see through me.

That night, Jeffrey and I fought, and I gave in as I had so many times before, telling him sick stories to avoid anything worse. The next morning at breakfast when everyone else was having fellowship, I kept to myself and felt very much as I looked—beaten down and depressed.

It wasn't long before Jeffrey returned to his old ways—playing mind games and asking me to sleep with other men. He withheld food from the children as a form of discipline, and I had to beg and argue with him to allow them to eat. He stopped attending church, and I gave up hope once and for all that he could change. I went to my pastor, Billy, and shared with him what Jeffrey had done and what he wanted me to do with other men. Billy agreed it wasn't of God and I had the right to leave him once again.

After another brief stint at the spouse abuse center, the church helped me find a house, and the children and I moved in with just a few plastic bags of clothes since Jeffrey refused to give us any of our belongings. However, the day after we moved in, we came home to find that the church had snuck in and furnished everything for us. The entire house was full of food, beds, and everything else we needed. The Lord had provided where Jeffrey had been spiteful, and with the church surrounding me, I had some hope that this would be the last time we would have to leave this man.

Every Sunday, I continued to go to church, and on Wednesdays, I watched the children so others could attend services. Before long, the children in our neighborhood were piling into my van to go to church on Wednesday nights. I was on fire for the Lord, and Jeffrey was angry that I had found happiness and continued in the church when he had stop attending.

Although I refused to go back to him, I allowed Jeffrey to see Tara sometimes. He said that the only way he would pay money for child support was if I agreed to keep it out of the legal system and allow him to pay me directly. I saw no harm in it and agreed. So every month, I had to take the trip out to his house in the country, where he would tell me I was still his wife and he expected me to perform my wifely duties before he handed over his money.

If I complained about him treating me like a prostitute, he would threaten to take Tara since he knew how afraid of the court system I was. These monthly trips were a source of great shame and a dark spot in an otherwise shining time in my life. But I thought I was doing what I had to do to provide for my children.

*

Now that my life was fulfilled in so many ways, I had every reason to go back to school. I returned to the same state counselor through Vocational Rehabilitation to inquire about a community college. I wanted to attend the University of Louisville, but I still couldn't read well enough and had very little knowledge of math.

In the beginning, I wanted to be a writer, but like most college students, I changed my mind and soon applied to the human services program. It seemed to be a more sensible path, and after all, I recalled being a little girl standing in the middle of the housing projects and promising myself I was going to make a difference for people who were hurting.

For more than a year, most of my classes were pass–fail. College was my life, and with every class, I became stronger. The human services program offered studies in the social work field, and although it took a master's degree to become a social worker, I attended and passed every class needed for an associate degree except for math.

I kept my grade point average right at or above 3.0 despite having to drop the lowest-level math classes over and over. I loved psychology and sociology, and with all the therapy I was receiving alongside my studies, I began to believe it should be a part of everyone's mental health plan to learn how the mind operates and what happens to the body and mind while under stress.

It was the highlight of my life, and God provided the endurance. For three years, I rotated between school, church, and my children, and I could not have been more thankful. In the church, I found the family I had always longed for, and I truly believed that if God was for me, who could be against me? But the events that unfolded next would test my faith in a way that even a harlot like me never could have prepared for.

# CHAPTER TWENTY-TWO

# Last Loss of Innocence

The visits to Jeffrey's house to collect child support continued to weigh heavily on me. I approached each visit with increasing dread and walked away with increasing guilt. I knew I couldn't truly embrace all the other blessings God had placed in my life while I was still degrading myself each month to receive the support that my freak of a husband owed me. So I made up my mind once and for all that no matter the cost, I was going to ask for a divorce and wasn't going to do the things Jeffrey demanded of me in exchange for child support. He would bring the money to me, and that was that.

It was a sunny day, and all the kids were off playing at a friend's house. I had been taking care of myself and was wearing makeup and dressing in the cute clothes I used to envy in my girlfriends. I had put on weight so that I no longer looked like a bony street rat, and my skin was tan from many peaceful hours in the sun. I felt pretty for a change.

However, my financial burdens were getting the best of me. Although I had been receiving some food stamps to pay for food, other bills were coming due, and I depended on child support to pay for extra food, clothes, and utilities. Jeffrey hadn't called in a while, and I had put off confronting him for child support as long as I could. But I was tired of being broke, and I didn't want to involve other people in my financial troubles, as doing so had led to so much strife in the past.

So I took what money I had left and bought gas for the forty-mile trip. It was already evening, and I took the expressway so I could hurry and get this over with before it got dark. I hated going out to that house yet again, but this time, I was going to stand my ground and finally be free. I would ask for a divorce and my child support, and I was not going to do anything for it that I didn't want to do.

Forty-five minutes later, I was pulling into the long driveway and starting to feel queasy as I saw the lights that looked like eyes shining out from the glass front of the house. I couldn't help but think about how isolated this place was and how alone I was. But I needed the money and needed Jeffrey out of my life, and this was how it was going to happen.

I got out of my car and left the keys and my purse inside, as was our custom in the country. I walked up the gravel driveway—gravel that I had purchased years before—and knocked on the front door.

"Come on in," Jeffrey called.

I let myself inside and sat down on the chair closest to the door. Jeffrey was sitting on the couch and began asking how I was doing and what was going on. These would have been innocent questions from anyone else, but with him, he was looking for information he could use against me. Finally, he dropped the act and asked directly, "Are you seeing someone else?"

"That's not really any of your business," I said. I refused to tell him anything about my life and instead tried to shift the conversation so I could get out of there as fast as possible.

"You know why I'm here, Jeffrey. I want my child support."

He crossed the room and handed me a wad of money. I felt uneasy and nervous as he stood over me. I could tell he was mad and wanted to talk some more, but my sense of dread was growing so much that I wanted out immediately—the divorce conversation could wait. But before I could stand up, Jeffrey reached over and locked the front door.

"I can't stay, Jeffrey," I said, trying to sound calm. "I have to get back to the kids."

"No, b——, you owe me, and you're going to pay."

"I owe you nothing," I said. "I'm not going to do anything for this money."

I got up to head for the door, but he stepped back toward me and shoved me back into the chair. He unzipped his pants and forced his exposed crotch in my face, screaming at me to pleasure him. I struggled to get around him and fought to try to make my way to the door. Then he grabbed me and pinned me back against the chair, and his grip was so strong that I couldn't fight him off.

With every breath, I choked on the smell of his body odor—the same rank stench that had tried to warn me away from him the first time I saw him at Sugar and Spice. I sobbed as I pushed and flailed and kicked—anything I could do to get away. But it wasn't enough.

He managed to wrestle me to the floor and screamed at me to take off my clothes. Memories of his threats to kill me and hide my body in the well pulsed through my mind, and I did as I was told. Then he forced himself on me as I begged, "No! Don't hurt me! I'm not going to do this! No! No!"

But no pleading would get him to stop. As he continued to have his way, I turned my head so I didn't have to see his face. He looked like a completely different person; all the color had left his face, and he was slobbering. His entire demeanor was of another spirit; he was more evil than I had ever seen him. I truly began to believe I would not get out of here alive.

When he was done, he got off me and began to cry himself. "No one loves me," he moaned. "No one has ever loved me."

I started pulling on my clothes and knew if I was going to get out, it would be now, while he was weak. I glanced at the door behind him and then looked at him, now sitting in the chair just by the door. I knew I had to do something quick while he was preoccupied with his tears. So I leaned into him and put one arm around him as if to comfort him while I reached over the chair and quietly unlocked the door.

He was crying and telling me that he had never been loved. Pretending to sympathize with my rapist, I said, "I feel your pain." Then, when I was sure he was distracted, I darted around the chair and swung the front door open.

With every ounce of strength left in me, I ran out the door and down the driveway to my car. Thanking God my keys were still inside, I started the car and backed down the driveway as fast as possible. I didn't look back until I was at the very end of the driveway, and then I saw him standing in the doorway of the house with his hands on his hips.

By the time I made it to the main highway, I wanted nothing more than to get back home and as far away from the country as I could. I was shaking and crying the whole way and couldn't believe what had happened. I had been pimped out as young as sixteen, but never had a man forced himself on me like this. I could always walk away from having to have sex, even if it meant taking a beating for doing so.

I had the money Jeffrey had given me in my pocket, but was it worth it? Every dime I spent of it would come with the memory of what it cost.

That night, I went home and was never the same again. I wanted to die. My brother insisted that I get a protective order against Jeffrey, and I lived in terror of not only facing Jeffrey again, but also going back to the place I feared most: the court system. A couple in my church recommended a Christian lawyer, and I started seeing counselors and social workers again.

Most of all, I turned to God and poured out all my devastation to him. I was sure no one was going to believe me, but at least I knew that God was on my side. However, being the young Christian I was, I was not prepared for the second act of betrayal that was about to come my way.

*

I took my broken soul to God and asked him to give me the strength to get through this process. I continued to attend church, and no matter what I needed, my Lord provided. I praised and prayed and greeted my fellow brothers and sisters as if nothing had happened. When church was over, I shook Billy's hand and told him that I had enjoyed the sermon and would see him Wednesday night. He smiled and thanked me.

Later that week was my court date to get an emergency protective order against Jeffrey. I was a bundle of nerves and sick to my stomach at the thought of having to relive that horrible night. My social worker sat next to me while we waited for Jeffrey to arrive, and part of me wanted him not to show up while the other part of me wanted him to hurry so we could get this over with.

But he did show up, and I immediately looked away and put my head in my hands. As I hid and waited for something else to happen, my social worker asked, "Mary, who are the man and woman with Jeffrey?"

I looked up and couldn't believe my eyes. It was my pastor, Billy, and the Christian counselor who had counseled Jeffrey and me for months. I had no idea they were coming, and by the way they avoided my eyes and sat down with Jeffrey, it was clear they were there to support him, not me.

I was shocked. How could it be that Jeffrey didn't even go to church anymore and yet my pastor and counselor were there to stand against me? I hadn't done anything that I could think of for them to betray me like this. My heart broke, and my whole worldview started to crumble right there in that courtroom.

Although the judge refused to hear their testimony, their presence in the courtroom was enough to destroy me. Jeffrey knew what he was doing. He knew my belief in God was all I had, and him bringing those two people made me feel as if God was on Jeffrey's side.

I barely remember getting through my testimony, and then I went home, nearly as broken and devastated as I had been the night of the rape. Both the church and state had abandoned me in favor of this man, and I had nowhere else to turn.

That Sunday and many others, I did not return to church. I went on to pursue my divorce, and as much as I tried to persevere through school, I was such a mess that I started failing my classes and was forced to drop out for a semester.

Several months later, Pastor Billy visited my house and asked me to come back to church. He even brought another ex-Vagrant to try to convince me. I asked him how he could come to testify against me and what he could possibly say that I had done wrong. He said he wanted to try to help save my marriage, and when that didn't soothe my anger, he claimed that he had been subpoenaed and had no choice but to come to court.

I didn't believe him. Besides, even if what he said was true, he should have warned me somehow. I had shaken his hand at church not days before, and he had let me leave in ignorance. None of his answers made sense, but even though I no longer believed or trusted him, I tried to return to the church just as I had returned to everything that ever hurt me. I wanted back what I had lost in God and didn't know how to get it.

I went to church the next few Sundays, but it was never the same. I tried to attend other churches but could think of nothing other than how I had been betrayed. The devil was hard at work, and I was convinced that he had won. I began to go out to bars and nightclubs where they played the blues, trying to let music and alcohol soothe my aching soul.

But even though the church had betrayed me, I could not ignore the still, small voice within me. I had experienced God in a way that was real and had changed me forever, and no sexual assault or courtroom drama could take that from me. So even though I couldn't bear to be a part of a church body, I would still sometimes visit a Catholic church late after a night at the bar when no one else was there. It was open 24/7 to allow wandering souls like mine to pray at all hours, and I spent many nights sitting alone in the pew in tears crying out to God and trying to figure out where to go from here.

# CHAPTER TWENTY-THREE

# My Dream Job

After the divorce from Jeffrey was finalized, I found the strength to re-enroll in school. Although I still couldn't grasp the math required to graduate, I was on the dean's list and made high enough grades in my other classes that I was often excused from having to take the final exams. By 2001, I had earned enough credits to look for work, and it wouldn't be long before I found my dream job.

I initially applied to the state to become a food stamp worker, but instead, a private agency hired me to work with first-time parents to teach them how to care for and bond with their babies. I was thrilled. I knew what it meant not to bond with your children and the consequences of it. As I trained for the job and learned more about the program, I wished I had had this kind of opportunity when my children were born.

I was forty years old and starting my first professional job, and I could not have felt more out of place. At the seminars and workshops my boss sent me to, I sometimes had to run out of the room to go to the bathroom and cry. It was bittersweet to learn what had gone wrong in my own childhood and in my efforts to raise my children. I wished I had known all of this information as a young mother, and it was also overwhelming to be reminded that even the worst parents really did love their children—meaning that, even in their neglect, my parents had loved me as well.

Unlike when I worked at the Riverside Saloon, I now had God in my life to help me work through my confidence issues. Every morning, I started the day by praying to ask God for wisdom and guidance to be the best family support worker I could be. And I did find a lot of success. I ended up working for multiple agencies and was on the front line in my field. Relating to clients was my strong point. I could communicate with them very well since I too was a parent who had once tried everything to get it right.

The only hindrance to my work during this time was a persistent pain in my back that sometimes flared up so badly that I couldn't sleep or even think straight. I don't know why, but I kept thinking I had a tumor on my spine. However, without having any kind of X-ray or other proof to back it up, people would just laugh at me whenever I shared my self-diagnosis.

Once after an episode of not being able to sleep for several days, my sister-in-law took me to the doctor, and I told him about the tumor I thought I had. My appearance must have been haggard and drained after days of fighting pain, so he too looked at me like I was crazy and dismissed me as a drug seeker.

My physical weakness got so bad that Jeffrey managed to work his way back into my life one last time. It all started sometime between me finishing school and getting my new job, when Tara was about nine years old and she came to me asking to see her father.

It had been more than a year since we had seen or heard from Jeffrey, and my heart broke as I looked at my daughter. She was an ideal child and was excelling in school, and I didn't want to deny her anything in life. So I said, "Oh, baby girl, Mama don't know about that. I'll have to think about it."

I agonized over it for a week and finally decided to call Jeffrey to let him know Tara wanted to see him. I felt I had no right to keep her from her father, and I worried she would resent me if I didn't let her see him.

So once again Jeffrey had his foot in the door. At first, it was just me arranging visits between him and Tara. But then when Christmas came around, he showed up with several thousand dollars' worth of gifts, and I knew he was grooming us again to depend on him.

Soon it was back to him begging me to get back together using all of his old tactics. He pushed and pushed, and I was so afraid of angering him like I had the night of the rape that I would say, "I don't know, I'll think about it," until he assumed we were together again.

As my family and friends began to learn that I was talking to Jeffrey again after he had raped me, they lost all respect for me, and I was so ashamed that I began isolating myself as well. I was no longer in church, and my family stopped taking my phone calls. My therapist was so upset about me letting Jeffrey back in that she stopped seeing me, and the state had to issue me a new therapist. Even Nana avoided me.

No one understood how afraid of him I was and why I didn't just stay away from him. To this day, I cannot say why Jeffrey had so much control over me. He had a way of convincing me that he was capable of pulling anything out of the hat and using it against me. But as long as I could keep him around, I felt I had control over being hurt. I didn't know how to explain to my loved ones that I felt safer when I was pacifying him than when I tried to run. I thought I could watch what he was doing and stay a step ahead of the fear.

Once Jeffrey was back, the crazy came with him. The push for sick sex was back. The constant pressure, smooth talking, and psychological warfare were back. And with it all came the anxiety that threatened to send me back to the hospital again. Jeffrey used all of this to his advantage and tried to convince me that if one of us was abnormal, it was me—the one who had acute anxiety and thought she had tumors on her spine.

He even tried to convince me that he didn't actually rape me. He would hold my face and force me to make eye contact with him as he said, "It didn't happen, Mary. You were having a panic attack and imagined it." But then other times he would put his arm around me and comfort me, saying, "You've been through so much; you've even been raped."

It was enough to make me question my own sanity. Had it actually happened? Had I done something to cause all these things that had happened to me? Maybe I was born to be what my mother, Dirty, and so many others would have me be. I had been an unwanted child, sold by one man and then given away. Abandoned and beaten and mistreated by those I loved. I truly didn't know what it felt like to be loved, nor did I know what self-respect was. All of my counseling told me to love myself, but that made absolutely no sense to me. What did make sense was enduring the abuse I had known for decades and finding a way to survive another day, even if it meant keeping an eye on my rapist.

*

At the end of 2002, a doctor finally examined me properly and found that I did have a tumor on my spine. In fact, he said it was the largest benign mass of its kind he had ever seen.

As the nurse showed me the tumor on film and explained that I would have to have emergency surgery or I would lose the use of my legs, I told her that I had known about the tumor for years but had been told it was all in my head.

She looked at me with pity and said, "It's not in your head, sweetie. You have suffered a long time."

My bridges were still burned with all my family members, and the only person who would claim me for my long recovery after the surgery was Jeffrey. By now, Ross was living with his father for the summer, and my twins were grown and gone. So Tara and I went home with Jeffrey, and he took family emergency leave to care for me. This was no great saintly act, of course; the whole time, he fretted that I was going to be paralyzed and he wouldn't want any more to do with me—which I would have been happy with. He talked about how burdened he would be if I became totally disabled.

For weeks, I lay in bed while my baby girl fed me noodles and soup made from the microwave. While Jeffrey sat on the Internet all day, I became even more depressed and dealt with more pain.

Finally, after being bedridden for months, I got to my feet and discovered my dogs had been left outside in the heat and one was full of maggots. I called my sister and asked her to tend to the dogs, and she agreed to take them to the vet. The house was a wreck, and I was still in so much pain that I could barely open a door. My hair was matted to the point that I couldn't get a brush through it, and if I tried, that hurt my back too. I paid my niece to brush it out, and it took half the day.

By now, I had lost my job. With all the pain and chaos in my life, I had fallen behind in my work and was forced to resign. I had lost everything—church friends, family, and my mind, and most importantly, I felt I had lost God. It seemed as if I had nothing to live for, and the pain was beyond any medication I could take.

That was when I began looking at Jeffrey's gun. I would open the drawer, take it out, and just hold it every once in a while. Then I placed it back, never really knowing why I was becoming so obsessed with it. I was depressed, to say the least, but now I was hopeless as well, knowing I was never going to be anything more than what others said I was.

One day, I found myself in the bathroom with every pill I had available, along with the gun. I placed the pills in individual piles spread out on the floor in front of me. And the gun was on the floor below them.

Tara was out playing, and Jeffrey was where he always was—at the computer. I picked up the gun, and it was already loaded. I reloaded the gun to put a bullet in the chamber. Several times, I placed the gun in my mouth before putting my thumb on the trigger. Then I would put the gun down and take several more pills to try to take away the fear.

Finally, after thirty minutes, I placed the gun back in my mouth and attempted to pull the trigger.

But the trigger didn't move.

I screamed when I realized what I had done. Jeffrey ran to the bathroom and took the gun out of my hands. It turned out that there was already a bullet in the chamber when I had reloaded it, and that had caused the gun to jam. To this day, I thank God for that.

I was admitted yet again to the psychiatric ward. This time, I was angry and felt I had nothing to lose. I wouldn't see Jeffrey or Tara even on visiting days. I cursed at the staff and refused to talk to them about Jeffrey and his manic hold on me. I was tired of telling people what they didn't want to hear and wouldn't believe anyway.

But all that pain and anger finally forced me to wake up and make a plan to leave Jeffrey once and for all. When I was released, I quietly began gathering everything I thought I could pawn, sell, or trade so that Tara and I could survive once we were gone. I slowly took our belongings to my brother's house and bided my time until we could follow.

Then, one day while Jeffrey was at work, Tara and I slipped away, and that night when he returned home, he would find that we had packed our things and left for the last time.

# CHAPTER TWENTY-FOUR

# Three Sixty

I would never speak to Jeffrey again but feared that he would hurt me or come for us in some way. With every waking moment, I worried.

Now that I had lost my job and spent months laid up on the couch, Tara and I were homeless. We moved around with different relatives who expected me to pay room and board, so I never had a chance to save money to rent our own place. We bounced around to different places until I felt we were becoming a burden, and then it was on to the next. Finally, we landed with my brother and his wife, and it was there that my life would begin to come full circle.

One day shortly after I moved in with her, my sister-in-law said, "You'll never guess who lives down the street from my daughter."

Her eyes were lit up with excitement, but I couldn't imagine whom she wanted me to guess. "Who?" I asked cautiously.

*"Dirty Dan!"*

I just stared at her for a moment and then said, "You're crazy. People have been saying he's dead for years. Or if he's not dead, he's in prison."

But she insisted that it was true and invited him over to

prove it. I don't think I really believed her until the man himself walked through the front door.

As tall as ever, Dirty Dan had to duck to get through the door frame. He had put on another hundred pounds and had more gray hairs and scars than ever, but he still had the same charming smile and smooth manners that could captivate a room. After a few steps, he stopped, put both hands on his hips, and smiled as he said, "Well, it's the Brat."

I got up from the chair I was sitting in and reached out to shake his hand. But he swept me up into a hug so tight that it hurt my back.

My family had always loved Dirty, and they all were excited to see him. My sister-in-law offered him something to drink as we all sat around the living room. It was 2003, and I hadn't seen him since my mother's funeral more than ten years before. We spent hours talking and drinking until one by one, everyone went to bed or left for one reason or another.

Dirty and I wound up sitting in the yard together that night and talking about old times. As I watched Dirty, something told me he would make sure Jeffrey didn't hurt me anymore, so I told him the whole story—where I had met Jeffrey, everything he had put me through, and all the way up to my last time leaving him.

When I finished, Dirty said, "I told you to never see your customers outside of business."

Although he was right, I couldn't help but reply, "Yes, and you also told me to sell myself when I was a little girl."

He had no reply to that.

For some reason, I was not afraid of Dirty like I was of Jeffrey. At least I knew what to expect from Dirty. He never told me I was crazy, and he would never allow others to hurt me—at least not anyone outside the club. I knew he would protect me, and since he was the reason I had lived the life I'd lived, I felt he owed it to me to help me get away from Jeffrey once and for all.

Dirty was living in an apartment owned by Mad Dog, the man who had beaten Rocky so badly. Once I scraped together enough money, I moved in next door to him with Tara and Ross. I thought I could complete the cycle by coming back to where it all started. As insane as it sounds, I felt that I had unfinished business with Dirty Dan and that I had to finish it so I could find myself.

The cycle continued further when I returned to the strip clubs as a dancer. I was in my mid-forties and had never dreamed I would be back here, but my life and my health weren't stable enough for a professional job.

Nor could I have ever guessed that I would start living with Dirty Dan again. After a while of living next door, we decided to move into one apartment to share the bills. For close to three years, we would live together but sleep in separate beds. Dirty paid his share of the bills while I worked in the clubs.

I truly believe Dirty was trying to make up for some of the wrong he had done to me. He was no longer a Vagrant, and although he still had the biker mentality in some ways, he never raised a hand to me. In fact, he endured a little bit of abuse from the ninety-pound girl he used to throw around the room.

In our relationship this time around, I began to tell Dirty what was on my mind, and I was determined he was going to listen to me instead of dismissing me as the mouthy Brat. One night, Dirty didn't want to hear what I had to say and went off to sleep, leaving me angry and frustrated in the living room. So I got a bucket, filled it up with water, went into his bedroom, and doused him with the entire bucket of water while he slept.

Being big and clumsy, Dirty had trouble hauling himself out of bed, so I left the room, filled the bucket again, and threw the second round of water at him.

"Damn it, Brat, stop throwing water on me! You're getting the bed wet!"

"If I can't sleep, nobody is going to sleep. You don't want to talk to me, Vagrant? You don't have to, but you're not sleeping."

At any time, he could have hurt me, but I knew he couldn't outrun me now that he was old and slow and walked with a cane. I would dare him to put his hands on me and remind him of what he had done to my life, blaming him for all my choices. I wanted to do worse whenever I recalled the days when he beat me.

Another time, he was sitting in the recliner, tilted back relaxing and drinking a beer. I wanted to talk again and he wouldn't listen. To this day, I don't know where the strength came from—and it hurt my back to do it—but I grabbed the foot of the recliner and tipped over him, the chair, his dog, and the beer so that the chair fell on top of him.

"Get up, Vagrant!" I taunted him. "You aren't so bad now, are you?"

I tormented him in every way I could, and he allowed me to vent my hurt. All of it built up until one night, I finally was able to get off my chest what had haunted me for all these years.

"Dirty, remember the time you gave me away?" I asked.

"No, I didn't, Brat," Dirty said. "I just told Rooster to carry you back to Louisville that day."

"You know, the last thing you want to do to me is tell me something that isn't true. The best thing you can do, Vagrant, is shut up and listen." When he didn't respond, I took a breath and said, "You were nothing more than a pimp who took advantage of little girls and young women. You should be ashamed."

When I was finished, Dirty went to another room in the apartment, and I let it go. He didn't ever say he was sorry, but something about confronting him so directly finally made me feel as though I had had my say. I sat at the kitchen table and cried, and knowing I was right, Dirty left me alone. We stayed together for some time, and the entire time, he paid his part of the bills, something he had never done with any other woman.

Dirty soon moved back to New Mexico to be with his mother, who was dying. Before he left, he wanted to bring Tara and me money as his parting gift. I was standing at the kitchen sink doing dishes when Dirty came in to say his last good-bye.

"I've got to go to catch my plane, Brat. I love you, and I want you to have this money."

With that said, he handed me a hundred dollar bill and then gave Tara a twenty. I told him to have a safe flight and said good-bye, and then Dirty Dan walked out the door for the last time.

After he had gone, Tara said, "Mama, my money has blood on it."

I looked down at the money he had given me, and sure enough, it had blood on it too.

"Hurry, get the bleach and hand sanitizer," I told Tara. Later, I learned that Dirty had gone to collect money from someone who owed him and had refused to pay. Once a biker, always a biker, I suppose.

I kept in touch with Dirty over the phone, and shortly after his mother died, he told me he had throat cancer and the prognosis wasn't good. He offered to fly me out to New Mexico to be with him while he was dying, but I couldn't bring myself to go to him. The thought of being with him and comforting him in his death confused me.

All I could remember was my pain and everything he had done to me. Dirty begged me to be with him in his death, but being with him for the last three or so years was never about loving him but about getting back at him and getting an answer to why my childhood innocence was taken. And I knew he would protect me from Jeffrey. My children cared for Dirty, and he was very good to my whole family, who saw him as one of their own.

When Dirty died, my family grieved, and his ashes were sent to me in a heart-shaped urn. I felt wrong having them, so I gave the urn to one of my brothers. Sometimes my brother and his friends would take out the urn, set it among them, and say they were partying with Dirty Dan.

Whenever I looked at the urn, it reminded me not of Dirty but of everything that had happened to me after I left him as a young girl up until now. I remembered the ice cream truck and who I was then—unwanted by everyone but a pimp. And the worst thing was that I was nearing my fiftieth birthday and was still dancing in the clubs, and I didn't feel all that different from that little girl roaming the streets of Butchertown.

# CHAPTER TWENTY-FIVE

# The Geriatric Stripper

Working in the strip clubs as a woman in your late forties is completely different from working there in your twenties. The biggest change is that the managers ship you off to day shift—a time of day reserved for junkies, alcoholics, and men coming in on their lunch hours. The men who frequented the clubs during day shift were a completely different breed from the nighttime clientele. They didn't come to drink and party but for their own perverse needs. They didn't care what you were or if you were attractive or not; you were just a body, a piece of meat. It didn't even matter if you were a geriatric stripper—and that's what I was now, a geriatric stripper.

More than thirty years after I started, I was right back where I was destined to be (or so I thought). Who was I to try and make it out? Who did I think I was to go to school and try to become something other than what I had been all these years? I was college educated and streetwise and had years of psychotherapy under my belt. But in so many ways, I was still that little girl at the ice cream truck. *What's it gonna take to end it?* I kept asking myself.

Although I was nearing fifty years old, I had somehow

managed to keep my figure. However, even after surgery to remove the tumor, my back hurt nonstop. I wore a corset to hide the fact that my scoliosis had gotten grossly worse, and I couldn't sit without excruciating pain. For that reason among many others, I desperately wanted a bartending job.

That was the other thing about being put out to pasture: All the old girls like me wanted to be a bartender because it was guaranteed money each day rather than depending on our looks and wiles to earn us tips from the day-shift men. As absurd as it was to covet anything in this dark place, we all coveted winning a bartending position, and so day in and day out, I danced for pennies while waiting for my big break to come along.

My day began at noon and lasted until eight in the evening when the second shift came in. There were never more than three to four customers in the bar during the day, so you hoped your mark would stay throughout your shift to spend money on drinks or buy lap dances. Some days I left with only two dollars after an eight-hour shift.

With Dirty Dan gone and no one to split the rent with, I moved out of the apartment and into my brother's backyard. I was living in one of three shacks he had built and paying him to run an extension cord out there so I could watch television or plug in a fan. Tara had moved away without telling me where she had gone, and I worried every day for her. I still had two family dogs that I refused to let go of because I felt I had lost everything and couldn't bear to let go of my children's animals.

In this fifteen-by-eight-foot shack, my bed was a workbench that had multiple blankets on it for padding. A net hung over the door to keep out the bugs, and I relied on my dogs to alert me if someone came through the alley while I slept.

I attempted to make the shack look as much like a home as possible. I had a broomstick mounted in the corner so I could hang up the clothes I washed in the house. Above my work-bench bed was a shelf that held plastic bins full of my clothes. Another shelf held my ramen noodles and canned soup, along with a cooler that I kept packed with ice to store my lunch-meat and soda.

On the other side of the shack was another workbench that served as my dressing table and a beat-up table that held my television and fan. On the floor were dog bowls for my minia-ture pincher and black Labrador. A cedar chest contained my valuables, including my children's school pictures and writings and notes for this book. After all that, I had maybe two by three feet left for walking space.

I refused to ask anyone for help and believed I deserved to be where I was. I was trying to earn enough money to pay rent and put down a deposit on an apartment, but I could never earn enough at the clubs to do so. I used to tell Jeffrey, "I would rather live in a shack on the river" than to live in his house, and now I was doing just that, since my brother's house was across the street from the river in the west end of Louisville. From the expressway, it looked like a junkyard, as you could see the three shacks all lined up among the garbage, tires, and broken-down furniture.

The backyard was cluttered with everything you could imagine. Carpet was laid out in the yard, and when it rained, you could smell the mold, mildew, and dog urine. Beer cans lay all over the ground waiting to be recycled. One of the other shacks contained a cheap sound system, and everyone would sit in the dirt drinking beer and partying through the night. Except for the trash on the ground, the yard actually looked a bit like a living room since my brother had decorated it with cloth-covered chairs that others had thrown out. There was even a refrigerator protected by a makeshift building made of plywood and tarps.

At these backyard hangouts, I ran into another person from my past: Regina. Regina had been my brother Richard's girlfriend in the 1960s; she used to be a stripper and had entertained me when I was a young child by showing me her costumes and teaching me dances like "The Jerk." She was in her sixties now, and was old and haggard, having lost all of her teeth and rarely brushing her hair. She was beaten down from all the drugs and alcohol she had consumed, and her face bore many scars from years of men abusing her. She was slow minded and hadn't a clue about her surroundings at times.

As I watched Regina now, I often wondered if this would be me in a few years since I had nearly repeated her lifestyle over the past few decades. I tried to have conversations with her, but she no longer made sense and babbled about anything. I felt sorry for her and hated the fact that everyone took advantage of her. But I never forgot the kindness Regina had shown me as a child, and I tried to repay her by showing her attention in her old age. Although she probably had no idea why I would be so patient with her, I listened to her ancient stories of the days when she too was a prostitute and "go-go girl." She was a constant reminder to me to get out of the industry, but even though I was living in a shack, I hadn't yet reached rock bottom.

Nearly every day for two years, my sister-in-law drove me to work and picked me up since I usually didn't earn enough to take a bus or cab. Although it was broad daylight when I arrived, the clubs were as dark as ever so that it took several moments for my eyes to adjust when I left the light of day to come into the darkness. I was the only dayshift dancer, so it was usually just the bartender and I there at first.

Every day, I made my way to the dressing room to apply makeup and pull together something provocative to wear. Once finished, I would rummage through my bag containing costumes and an extra pair of pumps and pull out a pocket Bible. Then I would spend the next half an hour or so reading about God leading the Israelites out of the desert. I couldn't help but relate as I sat in the desolate place that was a downtown strip club in the middle of the day, and after I prayed for forgiveness for what I was about to do, I would pray that I too could experience that kind of deliverance.

However, even as I prayed, I felt such salvation wasn't for someone like me. I had tried everything I could think of to change my life. Yet here I was continuing to make the same choices leading me back to the bars. I couldn't hold a real job because I needed more surgeries on my back. No man would have me besides an abuser, no employer would have me besides a strip club, and no landlord would have me besides a shack. Why would I expect that the God of the universe would bother with a woman like me sitting in the back room of a strip club?

In August of 2010, a few weeks before my fiftieth birthday, my neck and part of the back of my head had been shaved after yet another surgery. When I got to work, I put on my makeup as usual and then pulled my remaining hair over the bald spots to try to mask the signs of my ailing body. But when I inspected myself in the mirror, I began to cry as I got a glimpse of the little girl who had started working at these clubs more than three decades earlier. Through my tears, I pulled out my pocket Bible and tried to find anything to read that would give me hope.

In spite of Jeffrey's presence, the happiest time in my life

was when I had been in church, and I would have done anything to get back to that. However, after my pastor betrayed
me, I trusted no one when it came to God. I refused to get
close to anyone because I was afraid they would take God
away just as Pastor Billy and Jeffrey had. So although I loved
God, I kept my relationship with the Lord to myself, never
wanting to expose myself to the hurt that even God's people
could bring to my life.

Once I finished reading the Bible, I found my way out into
the club and greeted the bartender. Instead of the usual small
talk, she said, "Did you hear I'm leaving soon?"

"Really?" I said. I asked her what was next for her, but in my
head, all I could think of was that my relief had finally come. I
was next in line to become a bartender, which meant I was
guaranteed to make twenty dollars a day instead of the cents I
was making now. Maybe I could finally save for an apartment
and start to turn things around.

When the manager showed up that night, I pleaded for the
position, and he promised that it was mine. By the end of my
shift, I had made six dollars, which was only enough to pay my
sister-in-law for gas to pick me up. I didn't care though. My
days as a dancer were numbered, and bartending would be my
salvation.

The following day, a Thursday, I went through the same
drill of applying makeup, curling my hair, and adjusting it to
hide the shaven areas and the scars and stitches in my neck.
After Bible time and saying a little prayer, I went out to sit on a
barstool and wait for customers.

Throughout that day, the only times the door opened were
when one of us went out front to smoke. I spent the day
talking to the dayshift bartender and not making a dime. Once
my shift ended, I called my sister-in-law to tell her that I would

be staying for night shift since I hadn't made money for gas or cab fare.

The night shift girls started to clock in, and the bartenders were changing shifts. A customer or two straggled in from the streets, but now I had competition from younger women. At least they would draw in customers so perhaps I could make enough to pay for the gas home and back the next day.

I greeted one of the younger dancers, and she said, "Hey, Bell, how have you been? Did you make any money today?"

"No, sweetie, not a dime."

She then got up onstage, and as I watched her dance, I worried that she would fall from the pole.

Ten o'clock rolled around, and I still had not made enough money to pay for my way home. The door opened, and I looked around, hoping that it was a customer. However, it was two young women wearing jeans and modest T-shirts. They looked like college students. I wondered if they were looking for a job, and they looked so innocent that I wanted to tell them to turn around and leave. The way they were glancing around made it clear they had never been in a strip club before, and I knew that if they got drawn in, they may never get out, just as I had.

I wanted to tell them that if they had come for a job, they should change their minds and get out while they could. But then it hit me. I had seen these women before—or at least ones like them. They were part of a church group that served food to dancers in the clubs. I had met them a year before and thought how different they were from the church people who used to stand outside and protest, the ones who always made me feel so ashamed that I hid my face when I went to and from work. These young women had talked with me and prayed with me, and it was the first time (aside from my pocket Bible) that I had experienced God in these God-forsaken places.

Excitement raced through me, and I yelled out, "It's the church ladies!"

I shouted so loudly that they were visibly startled, but when their eyes fell on me, they smiled. "Yes, we're the church ladies," one of them said.

Desperate, I ran over to them and said, "Look! I need prayer. Look at my neck." I turned around and lifted up my hair to reveal the fresh scar from my surgery. "I just had surgery, and I need prayer badly. Can you pray for me?"

The girls were happy to pray for me, and as we bowed our heads, a customer left the stage to join us. It was so strange to pray with a customer—someone whom I would normally prey upon just as he preyed upon me.

After we prayed, the girls asked me, "Are you hungry?"

"Famished," I said, as I hadn't eaten all day and had only noodles waiting for me back at the shack.

I followed them to the club next door, where other women from the ministry had set up food along the bar. They invited me to take as much as I wanted, but I felt a sense of shame as I loaded up a plate and continued to try to talk to them with my mouth half full. The girls could tell I was desperate, and I was—in more ways than one. I think they were shocked that I hadn't avoided them; most of the dancers distrusted them, or accepted the food without talking to them. But I found myself nearly as hungry for their company as I was for the meal they had brought.

The girls told me their names were Julie and Kassie and asked me mine. I replied, "Well, they call me Bell, but my real name is Mary."

We went on to talk about how many clubs I had worked in and for how long. I continued to eat, one plate after another, and not wanting to appear rude for eating so much of their food, I answered all their questions. I told them all about the Vagrants and Dirty Dan putting me to work in the industry when I was just a kid around 1976. I talked about all the money that you could make back then and how girls rarely made money today, especially a geriatric stripper like me. I could tell the girls wanted to laugh when I used that term, but they held it in.

When we stepped outside so I could smoke, Rachelle, the woman who had started the ministry, asked me, "If you had the choice, would you leave the clubs?"

Surprised, I answered, "Well, yeah." Privately, I thought, *Who wouldn't want to leave this hellhole?*

"What's holding you here?" she asked.

I had a lot of answers to that question—money, my back, the shack, my pitiful résumé—but somehow none of them seemed sufficient at that moment. "I don't know," I said honestly.

"If you had the opportunity, would you leave?" she continued.

"I have never been asked that," I said, giggling nervously, and then I stared at the concrete as cars blew their horns at us as they passed by the club.

Before they left, we exchanged phone numbers and they invited me to church with them that Sunday.

Before they walked away, the memory of the customer praying with us earlier that evening came back to me, and I said, "Hey, what did you think about the customer who left the bar and joined us when we prayed?"

They looked at me confused, and Julie said, "I don't remember any customer."

"He was right there next to us. Didn't you see him?"

They still didn't know what I was talking about, so I let it drop. I couldn't help but think about the angel who had visited me when I was a little girl, but I tucked the thought away with all the other unreal and unbelievable things I had seen and heard in my life.

In the wee hours of the morning, I made a little more than ten dollars, enough to finally go home. I was so excited about my new friends that it wasn't until I was back at the shack that it hit me: What had I just been praying about and reading about in my pocket Bible? I had read about God parting the Red Sea, overthrowing kings, bringing down city walls, and dying on a cross to deliver his people from evil.

Although I had prayed that God would deliver me too, I never thought I would see something as dramatic as those miracles, especially not for someone like me. After all, why should I expect God to come down from heaven and come into a strip club of all places? But then again, I had prayed for God to intervene, and all of a sudden, Christian women appeared right in the middle of my nasty, sin-filled workplace. What if those girls—who had come into a place where you'd least expect God's people to go—had something to do with a harlot's cry to her God?

Perhaps it was all a coincidence. But then again, maybe it wasn't. I tossed and turned on my workbench bed as my heart swung between excitement and doubt. I had tried to leave the industry so many times, only to return again, and I had no reason to expect this time would be any different. Still, although I thought I had seen it all, the presence of those Christian women in a strip club had proved me wrong. And their questions about what was holding me there made me wonder what else I might have been wrong about all these years.

\*

After my encounter with the church ladies on that Thursday night, my manager told me I would start my bartending job the following Monday—on my fiftieth birthday. Here it was: my chance to earn guaranteed money even if not a single customer came in, and to have a position behind the bar where I would be safe from men groping and seeking cheap thrills.

But as I was trained on the register and all my new responsibilities, I didn't feel the excitement I expected to feel. Most girls, especially those on day shift, would have done anything to get this job, but the thought of it didn't bring me the same joy it had even two days before. The phrase *It's time to go* kept playing like a refrain in my head, but I didn't see how that could be true, not when I had finally gotten the bartending job and when there was no new job or place lined up for me outside the club.

Sunday came around, and although I was nervous and tempted not to go, I responded to Julie's and Kassie's texts and joined them for church. It had been years since I had heard a sermon; in fact, the last one I had actually listened to was by the ex-Vagrant Billy just a few days before he betrayed me in court.

As the service progressed, I tried and failed to keep my composure. Everything about it stirred something deep in my heart. Hearing God's people sing the songs I had sung only in private for years. Hearing God's words spoken out loud after only squinting at them in the darkness of a strip club dressing room. Hearing anew that God was real and present in every breath we took, and wanted desperately for his people to repent and come to him. I left the service knowing that God still loved me and that hope was at hand.

After church, I talked to Rachelle, the founder of Scarlet Hope, which I learned was the name of the ministry that had brought me food that Thursday. Although she didn't know all the details of the war going on in my heart, her advice to me was exactly what I needed to hear: "We are not here to tell you to leave the clubs, Mary. We are here to tell you that there is a choice, and it is yours to make. God will sustain you, if you make the choice to leave."

I said nothing to her comment, but the word *choice* weighed heavy on my heart as I went home that day. I had never really felt like I had a choice when it came to working in the sex industry—not when my circumstances always seemed to lead me back there. Not when Dirty Dan dropped me off at the picture booths that first time. Not when I came back to Louisville with no support system and no skills other than selling my body. Not when I left abusive husbands and had children depending on me.

What a gift from God it would have been to be free—really free of the sex industry. To have that choice I had never thought was mine to make. A few days before, I had thought my breakthrough was in bartending, but it seemed that God had much bigger plans for me than I had had for myself.

I knew what I had to do. The only question now was if I would have the strength to do it.

CHAPTER TWENTY-SIX

# Salvation

The day was Monday, August 16, 2010, my fiftieth birthday and my first day as a bartender. God had heard my prayer to leave this place, and now I had to choose whether I was going to respond. There wasn't much business that day, which gave me plenty of time to think about all I would leave behind.

As the minutes ticked by, my resolve became stronger and stronger, and I started to envision my simple plan of escape. I had to get out. God had something for me; I could feel it with my entire being. I wanted God's love again and had to trust him with my broken soul, or I was going to die in this place. The road I had traveled had worn out more than my shoes, and as the Holy Spirit spoke to my heart, I knew a life-changing event was about to happen.

What I didn't know was that a strange peace would sustain me my whole last day working in the sex industry. Somehow I knew—totally knew—that I would not be back this time. I had been trapped within my own mind for so long, but God had spoken to my heart and I had never been so sure of anything in my life. God had given me the choice to leave this lifestyle, and I had no excuse as to why I should stay. Where before I had

266 | MARY FRANCES

been held down by a pimp or the fact that I was uneducated or lacked self-esteem or had children who depended on me, now God had come into the clubs to lead me out, just like all the stories I had read and longed for in my pocket Bible.

But why me? I asked myself this question over and over again as I thought about all the years behind me and everything I had survived. I was an adulterous woman who had depended on the world and its evils to provide for my needs. My heart broke as I looked into the faces of the dancers I was leaving behind because I saw so much of myself in them.

But God had come for me, and just as Jesus's disciples dropped everything to follow him, it was now my time. I think I know how they must have felt. The stakes were high, but nothing else mattered but God. I now had a concept of faith, a tiny seed that continues to grow with each passing day. But first, I had to make my way out of this place to receive God's blessings, promises, and protection.

I was scheduled to open the club the next day, but at the end of my shift on Monday, I placed the keys to the building under the cash register drawer. I didn't want to tell the manager that I wasn't coming back; I didn't want to give anyone the chance to try to talk me out of leaving. Besides, I loved the other dancers like sisters and knew I would be leaving them behind in a place where I had seen so many lose so much.

I tried to slip out without anyone noticing, but before I made it to the door, the other girls stopped me and presented me with a birthday cake. Candlelight danced in the dimness of the club as they sang "Happy Birthday" to me.

I began to cry. They had done something so nice for me, and I felt as if I was abandoning them. But looking back, I wonder if God had given me this birthday cake as a secret celebration between him and me to mark my promise to him that I would leave this place forever.

When they finished singing, I dried my eyes, thanked them for their kindness, blew out the candles, and walked out the front door, never to return.

\*

My sister-in-law picked me up from work, and once home, I found my family and my dogs in the backyard waiting for me with another birthday cake. I tried very hard to be appreciative of their surprise, but the weight of what I had just done was starting to settle on my chest, making it hard to breathe. Something was dying inside me. The Bible says we must die to sin to experience true life in Christ, but I didn't realize that the dying part would be so heavy. Somehow I knew this day was going to mark a milestone in my life, but I had no idea what God had in store for me next.

I thanked everyone for the cake and returned to my shack to go to bed.

The next day, Julie and Kassie called and asked me to lunch. I hadn't been to a decent restaurant in years, and I felt ashamed the whole time we were there, as I knew I stuck out among them. My clothes were old, and the gray in my hair was peeking through the blonde.

After lunch, I invited them to visit me in my shack. I tried to fix it up and make things neat and clean before they stepped in. Julie's smile became fixed as her eyes wandered around and she attempted to hide the shock on her face. I was so ashamed and dragged her back out into the backyard, where I found her the best chair in the yard to sit in. She and Kassie told me about a Bible study Scarlet Hope did on Thursday nights, and I eagerly agreed to join them.

That Thursday, I joined the women of Scarlet Hope for

Bible study, and I found that there were more former dancers like me who had responded to God's call to leave the sex industry. We all had the same shame that we longed to shake, and after just an evening with them, I felt like I had come home after a long journey.

It turned out that Scarlet Hope was made up of women from several different churches all around the city who had been called to minister to and share the love of Christ with women just like me. It was amazing. The Lord was sending his servants to the forgotten places and forgotten people, and as a result, lives like mine were being saved.

After Bible study, Rachelle, the founder of Scarlet Hope, asked me, "So how long were you in the clubs, Mary?"

"The better part of thirty-five years, I think," I said.

She was shocked, and I think I was too, as I had never really stopped to add up the years. All I knew was that it began at an ice cream truck when I was fifteen, and now I was fifty. I had a lifetime of stories to tell, and my new friends were eager to hear them and pray over me.

For the next two months, my new family kept me busy as I told them my stories. It was dinner here and stories, lunch there and stories, a coffee shop and more stories. I was giving my testimony without even knowing it.

I even told my story at a gala where Scarlet Hope was raising money to help women in the sex industry in Louisville. I didn't even know what a gala was at first, but it turned out to be one of the most glamourous events I had ever experienced. It was in a beautiful old theater, complete with gold railings, a white-tiled entryway, plush carpet, high ceilings, and huge, beautiful chandeliers. Men were dressed in tuxedos, and all the women, including myself, were dressed in floor-length gowns. I barely recognized myself. The entrance hall was decorated with Scarlet Hope's logos and posters bearing statistics about the sex industry.

It made me nervous knowing that I had been among those statistics and was about to tell the world all about it. I had just left this life behind; how could I ever make others believe me or understand what it was like to be trapped in a place like the sex industry? Who was I to stand before God's people? Would they be able to see who I really was under all these frills?

After a delicious dinner served on tables filled with fancy china, fine linen, and beautiful candles, it was my turn to speak. As I approached the podium, the projector onstage changed to show an old photograph of me and Dirty Dan that I had provided to them.

In the picture, I was barely sixteen years old, and he was twenty-nine. I appeared to be anemic and looked every bit as young as the child I was. I weighed maybe seventy-five pounds and was four feet ten inches tall. There was a sad look on my face, and my body language spoke volumes.

Meanwhile, Dirty was sitting behind me with me between his legs. This picture was not of the bumbling old man I had tormented for the last few years of his life. It was Dirty as he had been in his prime—the one who had prostituted me and torn me away from my home and thrown me across the room if I displeased him. He looked just as he had in the 1970s, with his long hair, scraggly beard and mustache, and tattoos up and down his arms. On his face was a look of hatred and heartlessness.

Anger rose up in me as I looked at the little girl in the picture. Just a few months ago, I hadn't been all that different from her. When Scarlet Hope found me, I had been sitting on a barstool half-dressed and hungry, and was sure that that was where my life would end. Now here I was in this glamourous place among these glamorous people, and all the shame I carried with me like a scarlet letter threatened to keep me from opening my mouth. But I had no pimp or abuser here to silence me, and so, clutching my pocket Bible, I turned to face the audience and began to speak.

When I finished telling my story, the house erupted in cheers, and before the night ended, I shook a hundred hands and made new friends in Christ. And in so many ways, that was a picture of what my life was like in the coming months and years—moving from the barstool in a dingy strip club into the light of walking with God fully and completely.

It's not that life changed overnight or that things suddenly became easy. I qualified for disability assistance (because of my back) to help make ends meet, but I faced—and continue to face—the same types of struggles and temptations that followed me throughout my adult life. But before I trusted God to come out of the sex industry, fear was my constant companion—a sick best friend that I nurtured every day in the midst of my troubles.

However, the day I walked out of the strip club for good, I made the decision to embrace faith over fear. I began with only a tiny portion of faith, hoping that God could hear a harlot in the back of a strip club. A tiny portion of faith grew and doubled and doubled again. As the light of God shined, my faith grew. I came to realize that I am not a harlot wearing a scarlet letter; I am the prodigal daughter of a king.

Over the next few years, I made new friends who weren't felons, alcoholics, or downright heathens. My new sisters and brothers greeted me with godly smiles and left me with prayers and hugs, something that took years to get used to. They even offered to take me into their homes to help me escape the shack, but I refused to leave my dogs, as they were the only family I had left. Although it took some time and prayer, a local charity helped me find an apartment that would accept me and my furry friends. No more dancing shoes and no more shack for me.

I continued to join my Scarlet Hope friends at church, but they were confused when I chose to sit alone. I wanted to face God and praise him alone, and I couldn't shake my old fears that church people would hurt me like my old pastor had. It would take years and a lot of alone time with the Lord before I was convinced that I could be safe in God's house again.

As I write this nearly seven years after Scarlet Hope found me, I have not set foot in a strip club since my fiftieth birthday—at least not as a dancer. Instead, my calling has been to reach out to women who are where I once was by continuing to share my stories.

It's not enough for me that the little girl from that picture with Dirty Dan is okay now. At this very second, a human being is being bought, sold, traded, given away, and too many times dying at the hands of a perpetrator, pimp, or someone who is supposed to love her. Sometimes victims take their own lives because they believe death will be a relief from the hell they are living. If it hadn't been for Jesus, there were times when I would have done the same.

We as free people must be aware of the heinous evils that take place in our nation, maybe even in our own backyards. Even I was probably fifty years old before I heard the term *human trafficking*. I heard Dirty Dan call it *white slavery* once when he was discussing the law and prostitution with another biker, but I didn't know what the term meant. Like a small child, I absorbed the words and let them lay dormant in my mind as this life of darkness was being laid out for me to survive and testify about to others.

Although I was with Dirty Dan for only four years, from age fifteen to nineteen, the damage was done; those four years cost me the next thirty of my life. And the fifteen years leading up to encountering Dirty all but guaranteed that he could thrust me down the path he did. I was like so many other women who just drop in the strip club one night to make Christmas money—only to find years later that they have lost everything, including their family, friends, health, confidence, credit, education, and—all too often—their very lives.

Perhaps I could have just walked out of the club when I was sixteen like I did at fifty, and my life would have been completely different. But for years, it seemed there was always something in the way. Bikers. Bills. Lack of education. Mental health issues. Children to support. The sex industry had felt like salvation from all those things.

But the real barrier to leaving a place like the sex industry is the darkness that longs to reel you back in. The darkness that whispers that this is all you are and all you can depend on in life, even as it hurts you and threatens to smother your soul. This darkness had chased me all my adult life, even appearing as demons in my dreams.

Neither education nor a good job nor a good man nor a good support system can fight darkness. Only light can. And so what brought me out of the sex industry was nothing the world had to offer, but only what God did. Jesus offered light, hope, and freedom where there had been only darkness, despair, and slavery.

The experiences and journey I have survived once haunted me, but somewhere in my heart, I knew I had to survive, if not for myself, then for the sake of the innocent whom the world seems to disregard. I too was forgotten about. So many people saw no hope in me, but when Jesus heard my cry for help, he came for me. From all the way down in the pit of a dingy dressing room, I offered simple prayers—stumbling prayers and tearful ones, to say the least. He heard me and knew my heart, and he knows yours as well.

For whatever reason, I am alive and well and have God in my heart. I am no longer afraid and ashamed of who I am, where I have come from, or the many sinful things I have done, experienced, or witnessed.

There is a road yet to be traveled. But all of my pain was not in vain. As Romans 8:28 says, "And we know that in all things, God works for the good of those who love him, who have been called according to his purpose."

It is a blessing to share with those who are hurting and who feel—just like I did—that there is no way out or that they are alone. But I can say from experience that God is there in your darkness and wants you to overcome the evils of this world, when—not if—you face them.

My life will continue beyond this last page, so it's difficult to know how to end. So I'll leave you with the advice that Nana gave to me so many times but that I ignored until the time was right: "Just give it to Jesus."

Thank you for reading *A Harlot's Cry*.


If you would like to write to Mary, you can e-mail her at mary@330publications.com or visit her Facebook page at www.facebook.com/aharlotscry.


For media inquiries or if you are interested in Mary speaking at your church, conference, or event, please e-mail Jennifer Bell at jennifer@330publications.com.


If you are interested in reading this book for your book club, please visit www.330publications.com for discussion questions and other resources.

# THANK YOU

Thank you to our "dream team"—Ben and Ashley Willis, Allison Lutes, Rebecca Sterling, Katherine Gentzel, Ryan Bell, and Steven and Tina Thompson—for helping us transform this work from a manuscript into a book.

Thank you to Ricky Jackson, for being my walking thesaurus, spell-checker, and encourager who never doubted me.

Thank you to Grace Place, for giving me a home while I wrote this book, and to my roommate Lea McAtee-Debelie, for letting me make you late for work while I read it to you.

Thank you to Anthony and Amy Russo and Nancy Aguiar (kiss kiss, love love), for being our early readers.

Thank you to Alea Petersen, Kate Blanchard, and the other ladies at Scarlet Hope, for your teaching and support.

Thank you to Phyllis Arnold and the ladies at the Harvard Bible study, for your wisdom and encouragement.

Thank you to Sherri Churchill and Diana Sandman at A Woman's Choice, for defining forgiveness for me.

Thank you to Jan Butler, for teaching me about gratitude and humility.

Thank you to Michelle King, for listening to me read the book at 3 and 4 o'clock in the morning.

Thank you to Rocky, for being my big sister and keeping me safe in dangerous times.

Thank you to my nephew Garry, for being my first fan.

Thank you to my children, Terry, Mary Lynn, Ross, and Tara, for surviving me and surviving with me.

Thank you to Josh and Rachelle Starr, for trusting the Lord even when he led you to minister to the sex industry.

And thank you to Julie Wiegand and Kassie Krueger, for walking into the darkest places in Louisville.

MARY FRANCES is, by the grace of God, a survivor of human trafficking and the sex industry. Mary has made it her purpose in life to share her story—whether in print or on stage—to help others who are hungry, suffering, and forgotten, as she was so many times. These days, Mary loves to spend time with her children and grandchildren, tend to her garden, play the guitar, and look after the dogs and cats that always seem to find their way into her home.

JENNIFER BELL is a writer and editor with a decade of experience in higher education and book publishing. Jennifer is passionate about sharing the truths of God through stories and helping others do the same. She is the author of *A Warrior's Legacy*, a young adult fantasy series (for more about her writing, visit www.jebell.net). Jennifer lives with her husband, Ryan, in Louisville, KY, but all things considered, they'd rather be in Disney World.

Made in the USA
Lexington, KY
30 August 2017